SHAW [J. SHAW] THE LIFE GUARDSMAN • WIL WALLINGFORD KNOLLYS AND JOHN SHAW

Publisher's Note

The book descriptions we ask book-sellers to display prominently warn that this is an historic book with numerous typos or missing text; it is not indexed or illustrated.

The book was created using optical character recognition software. The software is 99 percent accurate if the book is in good condition. However, we do understand that even one percent can be an annoying number of typos! And sometimes all or part of a page may be missing from our copy of the book. Or the paper may be so discolored from age that it is difficult to read. We apologize and gratefully acknowledge Google's assistance.

After we re-typeset and design a book, the page numbers change so the old index and table of contents no longer work. Therefore, we often re-move them; otherwise, please ignore them.

Our books sell so few copies that you would have to pay hundreds of dollars to cover the cost of our proof reading and fixing the typos, missing text and index. Instead we let most customers download a free copy of the original typo-free scanned book. Simply enter the barcode number from the back cover of the paperback in the Free Book form at www.RareBooksClub.com. You may also qualify for a free trial membership in our book club to download up to four books for free. Simply enter the barcode number from the back cover onto the membership form on our home page. The book club entitles you to select from more than a million books at no additional charge. Simply enter the title or subject onto the search form to find the books.

If you have any questions, could you please be so kind as to consult our Frequently Asked Questions page at www. RareBooksClub.com/faqs.cfm? You are also welcome to contact us there.

General Books LLC™, Memphis, USA, 2012.

❧ ❧ ❧ ❧ ❧ ❧ ❧ ❧

A complete Book will be issued each Month, in a Fancy-Wrapper, price One Shilling, illustrated with a Frontispiece in Colours and Engravings on Wood. *Among those to follow, will be—* 2— THE EXPLOITS OF LORD COCHRANE. 3— THE VICTORIA CROSS IN THE CRIMEA. J 4— ,, ,, INDIA. *ml* 5— ,, ,, THE COLONIES, &c. 6— UNDECORATED MILITARY AND NAVAL HEROES. 7— GALLANT SEPOYS AND SOWARS. 8— DARING DEEDS AFLOAT—ROYAL NAVY. 9— ,, ,, ,, MER-CHANT NAVY & PRIVATEERS. 10—FE-MALE HEROISM IN WAR. LONDON: DEAN AND SON, Publishers, I6oa, FLEET STREET

Dean& Son will commence to issue on October ist, in a cheap and popi form, the first of a series of interesting works, entitled— SHAW, THE LIFE GUARDS-MAN, r pf " Oswald Hastings; or, Adventures of a (Queen's Aide-de-Camp,"

SHAW, THE LIFE GUARDSMAN

AN EXCITING NARRATIVE.

BY

MAJOR K NOLLYS, F.R.G.S.,

93RD SUTHERLAND HIGHLANDERS.

Honfcon:

DEAN & SON, 160, FLEET STREET, E.C.

PREFACE.

HE following sketch of the career of the Life Guardsman has been compiled with great care, but unfortunately there are few materials for a biography of the gallant trooper. As regards the anecdotes, &c, the author does not pretend to have given any which have not yet appeared in print, but only to have collected numerous incidents, and placed them under one cover. Among other writers, extracts have been taken from Siborne, Kelly and Gronow, and the authority has, in most cases, been formally stated. MAJOR KNOLLYS. *Sept.* 1876. THE LIFE OF SHAW. APTER I. ORPORAL JOHN SHAW, of the 2nd Life Guards, has ever been the favourite among the humble military heroes of the British army. Till lately the exploits of none under the rank of commissioned officer have been officially chronicled, and many deeds of the highest valour and self-devotion have, in consequence, passed into oblivion. The deeds of Shaw, however, constitute an exception. By all classes his wondrous deeds of daring are proudly remembered, and by those of his own position in life the name of the gallant Guardsman has been at least as much associated with the battle of Waterloo as that of Wellington himself. Indeed, in many popular

B panoramas of the great battle, it is the Corporal, not the Field Marshal, who is the most conspicuous figure. The explanation is simple. The mass of the nation are incapable of appreciating the marvellous combination of military talent in the Great Duke.

The courage, coolness, energy, and prowess of the stalwart Guardsman, however, excited and still excite the admiration of the educated and uneducated alike. Englishmen are proud of Shaw because he was essentially the embodiment of the national characteristics, in short, he was a representative man. The fact, too, that he did not survive the victory to which, in his sphere, he had contributed so largely, has invested his memory with a sentimental halo. We are not, therefore, surprised to learn that, in these days of commemorations and statues, Shaw has not been forgotten, and that his fame is perpetuated by the skill of the sculptor.

Of John Shaw's origin and early life little has come down to us. We know that he was born in the parish of Woolaston, in the county of Nottingham, in the year 1789; and as he described himself, on enlistment, as a labourer, we may assume that his parents were in humble circumstances. He appears to have been educated at the parish school. From childhood he evinced a pugnacious disposition, and the courage, afterwards so conspicuous at Waterloo, was evinced in the readiness of the boy to fight on the slightest occasion and against any odds.

It was a pugilistic age, and all classes patronized "the noble art of self-defence." Princes, peers, and officials of the highest rank flocked to see a prize-fight or a set-to with the gloves as eagerly as they now rush to a boat-race or Lord's Cricket-ground. The best-born in the kingdom, in those days, were proud of recognition by one of the celebrities of the prizering, and few men of fashion but studied systematically under one of them.

Shaw, as we have said, was, from his earliest childhood, ever ready with his fists. When only sixteen or seventeen, he had the audacity to challenge a strongly built man, at least three stone heavier than himself. The fight came off just outside his native village, Woolaston, in the presence of a crowd of spectators. The lad stripped, and, heedless of the disparaging remarks from all quarters about himself, walked confidently into the ring, and formally defied his adversary by throwing up his hat.

At first Shaw appeared thoroughly overmatched, and, notwithstanding his pluck and strength, was getting severely mauled, when a powerful-looking man elbowed his way into the ring, and, tapping the lad on the shoulder, encouraged him with the following words:— "Youngster, don't you give it up. The big un won't get the better of you, after all; he's hitting too wildly, and 's a deal too cheeky. Take my advice, back away from him, and fight slow, and you 'll lick him, as sure as my name's Jem Belcher."

The announcement of his name by the new-comer must have created a great sensation among the bystanders, and not a little have encouraged Shaw, for Jem Belcher was the hero of a hundred fights, beloved and respected by the whole sporting fraternity, and second only to Gentleman Jackson. So great was his fame and popularity, that not a young "blood" among the aristocracy but felt honoured at receiving a grasp from his muscular right hand.

Shaw, on learning' from whom the advice and encouragement came, seemed to gather fresh strength, and followed out the directions given him with such success, that in a few minutes he compelled his antagonist to give in.

A few months later Shaw, anxious for a larger arena, proceeded to London; and on the 15th of October, 1807, being then eighteen years of age, six feet in height, with fair complexion, grey eyes, light hair, and round visage, enlisted in the 2nd Life Guards. He was a remarkably large-limbed man, of great muscular strength, being evidently possessed of some education as well as of good character, for he was in due course promoted to the rank of Corporal, a grade which, in the Life Guards, is equivalent to that of Sergeant in other corps. We may here mention that, before he died, he gained half an inch in height.

Shaw, on joining the Life Guards, found himself quite in his element, for pugilism was much cultivated by the Household Cavalry, and very few months had elapsed before he was recognized by his comrades as a bruiser of the first water. His prowess soon stood him in good stead.

At the beginning of the century, as now, the soldier was exposed to the vulgar insolence of the lower classes, and was often saluted with cries of "lobster," "a shilling a day to be shot at," and similar silly chaff. Occasionally, the would-be wits got a severe lesson for their impertinence, and seldom was it more severe than the one administered by Shaw, under the following circumstances. He was quartered in Portman Street barracks (originally occupied by that Horse Marine sort of corps the Horse Grenadier Guards, subsequently a quarter of the Foot

Guards, and about twenty years ago demolished), when three strongly-built roughs assailed him with various uncomplimentary epithets. His blood was up in an instant, and before they could guess his purpose, the three jokers were sprawling in the gutter. Seeing themselves, however, three to one, they, on recovering their legs, set upon the young Lɪfe Guardsman. But they had

caught a Tartar, and in less than five minutes Shaw had given them such a drubbing, that they were obliged to take refuge in flight.

His fame as a boxer becoming widely known, Colonel Barton, a well-known patron of the ring, took him in hand, and introduced him to the Fives' Court, then the most famous temple of the art of pugilism.

Shaw was indeed a formidable novice. He stood upwards of six feet in his stockings, and his weight, when stripped, was fifteen stone, while the dumb-bells and sword exercise had developed the muscles of his arm, and given him a wrist strong and flexible as a bar of steel. To use the words of one of his most celebrated admirers, " His height, weight, length, and strength were of so valuable a nature, that, united with a heart which knew no fear, they rendered him a truly formidable antagonist."

At first Shaw was considered rather slow in his movements; but constant practice with the gloves with the best boxers of the day gave him the necessary quickness, and it soon became recognized by the professionals at the Fives' Court and Jackson's, that the young pugilist would ere long oblige them to look to their laurels. The public began now to take him up, and he justified their favour by defeating the celebrated Molineaux in a contest with the gloves. He had, however, like every novice, occasional failures. He came off conqueror in a figlr with the gloves with Captain Barclay, of Ury, the wellknown amateur pedestrian and boxer; but Barclay was avenged a few days after by Tom Belcher, brother of Jem Belcher, whose advice had stood Shaw in such good stead on the occasion of his first fight. The encounter was with gloves, and Shaw, notwithstanding his strength, reach, pluck, and skill, was soon disposed of by the veteran pugilist.

The first appearance of Shaw with ungloved hands in the prize ring was on the 12th of July, 1812, at Coombe Walden. His opponent was a West Countryman of the name of Burrows, who had recently fought a good battle of an hour's length with Molineaux, when the latter was at the height of his powers. Shaw adopted the retreating tactics of the renowned Cribb, and they proved completely successful. In seventeen minutes Burrows had been so badly mauled that he could not see his way from the ring, and had to be led off by his friends.

Shaw's fame as a pugilist was now firmly established; and he devoted all his spare time to increasing his skill and strengthening his muscles. By this means his naturally fine form became so magnificently developed, that he at one time used to sit as a model to Haydon the sculptor. Whether he fought any battles between 12th of July, 1812, and 18th of April, 1815, we know not. Most probably he did. At all events, on the latter date he appeared for the last time in the ring. Hounslow Heath was the scene of the fight, and all the roads leading to the destined battle-field were thronged from early morning by strings of carriages of every description,—men on carts, men on horseback, and men on foot, flocking to see the Life Guardsman display his prowess.

There was much excitement on the occasion, for a short time previously Shaw had boldly challenged all England for the championship. Besides, it was a double event, as proceedings were to be commenced by a set-to between Harmer and Skelton. These two fought a terrific battle of twenty-eight rounds, at the end of which Harmer was declared the victor. Shaw and Ned Painter then peeled and stepped into the ring. In appearance Painter was very inferior to his antagonist, for though he weighed thirteen stone, he was only 5 feet cjf-inches in height. Moreover, he had but that morning come out of the Fleet Prison, and could not, therefore, have been in good training. He was, however, no mean antagonist, and had many previous successes to look back upon. When quite a stripling he had shown much skill as a pugilist, and had fought and soundly thrashed a grown-up man of twice his strength, in the yard of the Swan Inn, Manchester. Subsequently, he had beaten a couple of Heavy Dragoons, quar-

tered at the same inn, who had annoyed every one by their bullying and swagger. Eventually he made a public appearance in Carter's Boxing Booth, Manchester. He must have been well thought of, for at Hounslow his seconds were Cribb and Oliver.

According to contemporary accounts, Painter set to work with great gaiety, at first seemed to hold his own very fairly, and gave and received terrific hits. Shaw's reach and weight, however, soon began to tell; and we are told that it was piteous to witness the punishment which Painter received, and the gameness with which he bore it astonished all beholders. Shaw soon seemed to do what he liked with his opponent, and gave him ten knock-down blows in succession. fainter was urged to give in, as he had not the faintest chance of victory; but he still struggled pluckily on till, at the end of a sharp twenty-eight minutes, he was quite unable to come to time.

This victory placed Shaw in such a position that, had he remained much longer in England, a fight for the belt with Cribb, the champion of England, must have taken 'place. Indeed, as we have said, even before the Hounslow Heath affair the Life Guardsman had openly challenged all England.

UT sterner work was yet in store for the gallant Guardsman. Napoleon had escaped from Elba, all Europe was gathering to crush him once more, and twelve days after Painter's defeat, Shaw and his comrades of the 2nd Life Guards marched from London to embark for Belgium.

The regiment, with the ist Life Guards, the Blues, and the ist Dragoon Guards, constituted the ist Brigade, commanded by Major-General Lord Edward Somerset. The head-quarters of this brigade was Ninove, and in that town and in its neighbourhood they were placed in cantonments. There they remained for about five weeks, the only incident to vary the monotony of their existence being a review, on the 24th of May, of the 1st and 2nd Cavalry Brigades by the Prince of Orange, followed, five days later, by one of the whole of the Cavalry

and Horse Artillery by the Duke of Wellington and Prince Blucher. This, however, was but the lull before the storm. On the 15th of June Napoleon crossed the Belgian frontier, driving in the advanced troops of the Prussians. The next day he attacked and beat Blucher at Ligny with the mass of his army, while Marshal Ney, with a strong force, endeavoured to gain the position of Quatre Bras.

Early on the morning of the 16th, orders to march reached the 2nd Life Guards, and shortly after 6 A.m. the brigade set off to Quatre Bras. It did not, however, reach the scene of action till after the last shot had been fired. On the 17th, the Duke of Wellington, learning that his prophecy—on the previous day, after seeing his dispositions, he had said the Prussians " would be most damnably licked "—had been fulfilled, resolved to fall back on the position of Waterloo. The retreat commenced about 11 A.m., and was covered by the cavalry.

At first there was no close fighting, only the artillery and skirmishers on each side being brought into play. The fact was that about midday a torrent of rain came down, and so saturated the ground, that rapid movements of cavalry were impossible. The town of Genappes consisted then mainly of one long crooked street, with few, if any, side entrances. After issuing from the town, the broad high road, by a gentle ascent, rises for about 700 yards. On the brow of this hill the Earl of Uxbridge had posted Somerset's brigade of heavies, and Ponsonby's Union Brigade, so called because it was composed of the 1st Royal Dragoons, an English, the Scots Greys, a Scotch, and the Inniskillens, an Irish regiment. Both these brigades were drawn up in column of troops. Close to Genappes were the 7th Hussars, and in support of the latter the 23rd Light Dragoons. Lord Uxbridge determined to check the progress of the French, in order to give the Duke of Wellington time for an orderly retreat. About twenty minutes elapsed after he had completed his dispositions, when suddenly a few horsemen galloped out of the street, and dashed into the leading squadron— Major Hodges's—of the 7th Hussars. They were at once taken prisoners, and found to be all drunk. They had, no doubt, pillaged the liquor-shops of Genappes. A few minutes later, some sixteen or eighteen French squadrons —those at the head being Lancers—entered the town, followed by the main body of Napoleon's army.

When the Lancers arrived at the end of the town, and saw the preparations made to receive them, they halted. The troops in rear not being able, from the turn in the street, to see what was the matter, kept pressing on, until the whole column became jammed into a solid mass, incapable of retiring, should such a movement prove necessary.

Lord Uxbridge, seeing that the enemy was undecided what to do, anxious to blood his men, and seeing that a favourable opportunity for doing so presented itself, ordered the 7th Hussars to charge. This regiment, full of ardour for the fight, and inspired by the presence of the commander of the Allied cavalry, who was also their own Colonel, rushed forward with the greatest impetuosity and resolution. Their horses were light, but so were those of their opponents. Moreover, the Frenchmen never advanced to the encounter, and it is an axiom in war that cavalry which receives an attack at the halt must be defeated. The British Hussars, however, failed, owing to the peculiar circumstances of the case. The Frenchmen had their flanks protected by the houses, they filled up the whole width of the road, they were prevented by the troops in rear from giving ground, and by couching their lances they opposed an impregnable *chevaux-de-frise* to their assailants, who failed to penetrate or drive back the mass, though they strove to do so most heroically. They persevered, however, for some time, and swordcuts and lance-thrusts were furiously exchanged during several minutes.

In the mean time, a French Horse Artillery battery had been firing with some effect on the rear squadrons of the 7th, and, profiting by the confusion thus caused, and by their own weight, the Lancers drove the Hussars back upon the 23rd Light Dragoons. The Hussars then rallied, renewed the attack, and forced the Lancers into the town again. It was now the turn of the Lancers to rally, and the Hussars once more gave ground. A second time, how-' ever, did the Hussars rally, and the fight continued with unabated fury.

Lord Uxbridge, seeing that the 7th were too light to accomplish anything against the French Lancers, sent an order for the Hussars to retire. Very deliberately the gallant 7th went about at the word of command; but the Lancers, wild with enthusiasm, and unwilling to lose hold of their antagonists, followed them up, and a fierce *melee* took place before the Hussars could extricate themselves, many men falling on both sides. At length the 7th shook themselves free of the Lancers, and, passing through the 23rd Light Dragoons, the shattered remnant formed up promptly in an open field by the side of the road.

CHAPTER III.

N the whole history of cavalry, there probably has never been so obstinately maintained a struggle between two bodies of horsemen as that which was fought out at the entrance to Genappes. Eoth sides displayed the utmost courage, and so persevering were the efforts of the British Hussars, that the French Lancers had good reason to feel proud of their success. Not only they, but the whole of the French troops in the town, were excited to a pitch of the wildest enthusiasm. Cries of "Forward! forward!" rent the air, and the Lancers, quitting the protection of the defile, advanced up the hill to attack the supports and complete the fancied victory.

Their elation was short lived. Lord Uxbridge had prepared a disagreeable surprise for them; and, causing the ist Life Guards to pass through the 23rd Light Dragoons, ordered them to charge. As soon as the ist Life Guards were clear of the Dragoons, the word "Charge " was given, the trumpets rang out, and, thundering down the ascent, the cloud of black horses plunged into the enemy's ranks with irresistible force. At their head rode Colonel Sir John Elley, commander of the Blues, but at the time serving as Deputy AdjutantGeneral.

Sir John had begun life as a private trooper, but by pure merit and hard service in many campaigns had attained the rank of Lieut.-Colonel of the Blues, Colonel in the Army, and Knight-Commander of the Bath. He could not look on and not join in the fray, and, riding well in front of the regiment, drew first blood for our side by cutting down two antagonists right and left.

The Lancers were unable to stand the fierce rush of our stalwart troopers on their powerful chargers, and the forest of lances was at once broken up, the unfortunate men who bore them being cut and ridden down as if they were so many children mounted on ponies. Horse and rider went down before the avalanche which smote them; the road was in an instant strewed with fallen men and horses, while those Lancers who kept their saddles at the first shock fled wildly to the rear, followed right through the town by the death-dealing foe.

It had been indeed a thunderbolt which Lord Uxbridge had launched at the rash Frenchmen who had dared to challenge the British horsemen to battle, and never during the remainder of the day were our cavalry seriously molested.

A comical incident occurred at Genappes, and caused great laughter among the 7th Hussars, who witnessed it. The ground was excessively wet and slippery, and in advancing to the attack of the French Lancers, the horses of several Life Guardsmen came down, sadly staining the handsome uniforms of their riders. For many years previously the Life Guards had seen no active service to speak of, and on this occasion they instinctively behaved as if they had been at a field day in Hyde Park. Now, at drill it was the custom for any trooper whose horse came down with him in muddy weather to go to the rear and get the dirt off before rejoining the ranks. To the intense amusement of old campaigners, such of the Life Guards who came down at Genappes calmly got up, and, in stolid conformance with regimental custom, led their horses calmly to the rear, instead of remounting and hurrying on to take part in the fight. Can there be a quainter instance of the effect of discipline?

Corporal Shaw and his comrades of the 2nd Life Guards must have felt much mortified at not being allowed to take an active part in the fighting of the 17th of June. As we shall see, however, they were destined to have on the morrow as much as would satisfy the greatest gluttons amongst them.

But to resume our narrative. The retreat having been accomplished, the troops bivouacked for the night on, or close in rear of, the position selected by the Duke. That position was a ridge of high ground running perpendicularly to the high road between Brussels and Charleroi, and divided by that road into two almost equal portions. Opposite this ridge, in the direction of Charleroi, was another ridge, about three-quarters of a mile distant. The descent from both ridges was easy, and the country, which was under tillage, was open except on the British ridge, where there were a few fences and hedges.

On the British right of the high road, and on the French side, near the summit of the ridge, was the farm of La Haye Sainte, while further to the right, and at the foot of the ridge, was the Chateau of Hougomont.

The night of the 17th was full of discomfort to the tired troops. The rain poured continuously, and at times came down in torrents, while from time to time lightning flashed and thunder roared, like an overture to the morrow's struggle. Without any protection from the pitiless storm, with no couch but the muddy ground, and, from the rain and scarcity of wood, having but a few smouldering watch fires, the troops rose next morning at daybreak stiff, numbed, and chilled.

Soon, however, the rain ceased, the vapoury masses, which had hung like supernatural shrouds over the destined battle-field, slowly rose, and formed a canopy through which, till just before the close of the day, the rays of the sun

were unable to penetrate. The troops took advantage of the improvement in the weather to clean their muskets, and the continuous discharge which resulted would have made one who heard, but did not see, think that a brisk skirmish was taking place. We may be sure that Shaw and his comrades busied themselves in cleaning the rust off swords and accoutrements, as well as in tending their horses and fitting them for the fatigues of the day.

Let us here pause for a moment to describe the 2nd Life Guards as they appeared on the morning of the celebrated 18th of June, 1815.

They were then, as they are now, all tall, muscular men, about six feet high, mounted on powerful black horses, none under sixteen hands high. The headdress was a brass helmet, with a blue and red woollen crest, and a tall straight scarlet and white plume on the left of the helmet. No cuirasses or jack-boots were worn, the jack boots being reserved for state occasions. The trousers were of blue mixture, with a red stripe down the outside of the leg. The coat was a double-breasted red coatee, and the sash round the waist was scarlet and yellow. The shabraques were of white sheepskin for the men and black sheepskin for the officers. The arms were long almost straight swords, pistols, and short carbines. It is worthy of note that the Life Guards were the first British troops who used rifles, eight rifled carbines per troop having been issued to them as early as 1680.

Let us now turn to the French Cuirassiers, with whom they were destined in a few hours to measure strength. These were the *ilite* of the French cavalry, and it was required of them that they should be six feet high, have served twelve years and in three campaigns, and be of good character. They wore steel helmets and steel back-pieces and cuirasses, the latter pigeon-breasted, and so strong, that unless fired at close they turned a musketshot. The Cuirassiers were almost safe against a sword, unless they were struck on the neck or limbs. They were, however, hampered by their armour, and could

with difficulty use their swords, except to thrust. They were armed with pistols, and straight swords some three inches longer than those of the Life Guards. Like the latter, they were mounted on powerful horses. They enjoyed the highest reputation for their almost invariable success, having rarely been overcome by hostile cavalry, and having on numerous occasions turned the tide of victory.

The 2nd Life Guards were commanded at Waterloo by c

Lieut.-Colonel the Hon. E. P. Lygon. They entered on the campaign 231 strong, and at the close of the 18th of June their numbers had been diminished by eightyseven killed—including three officers—and sixty-eight men wounded. They lost, in addition, 153 horses killed. The regiment may thus be said to have been almost literally annihilated, and the enormous proportion of killed shows how close and desperate was the fighting.

REAT as is the interest attaching to the battle of Waterloo, our purpose is simply to describe the part which Shaw and his comrades took in it. Early on the 18th of June, Corporal Shaw was sent in charge of a foraging party. When the first shot was fired about 11 A.m, he was at some distance from the field, but he promptly collected his men, and, hastening back, joined his regiment before the first charge.

About 2 P.M. Napoleon's grand attack upon the centre and left of the British army took place. It was made by four divisions of infantry, a cavalry division (Roussel's), composed of a brigade of Carabiniers a cheval and a brigade of Cuirassiers, a division of Light cavalry, composed of a brigade of Chasseurs and a brigade of Lancers, and seventy.four guns. The light division appears to have brought ur the rear in support

Of the four divisions of infantry, all but one brigade were on the English left of the main road. That one brigade attacked La Haye Sainte, and, driving in the skirmishers, afforded an opportunity for Roussel's horsemen to charge and cut up a large number of them before they could reach the crest of the British position.

The moment was critical; the whole centre appeared in danger of being forced; and Lord Uxbridge determined to relieve the pressure on our infantry by a charge of cavalry. He directed the Union Brigade under Ponsonby, which was drawn up to the left of the main road and behind the ridge, and Somerset's brigade, posted behind the ridge on the right of the main.road, to attack simultaneously.

Ponsonby's brigade was to deal with the infantry, Somerset's with the cavalry.

Somerset was ordered to keep the Blues in support, and Ponsonby the Greys.

In Somerset's brigade the 1st Life Guards were on the right, the 2nd Life Guards on the left, and the 1st Dragoon Guards in the centre. Shaw was in the centre of the left squadron of his regiment.

The whole of the front line of the French seems to have been composed of Cuirassiers, but we cannot speak posi.tively on this subject.

The Earl of Uxbridge, in order to encourage the British cavalry, and carried away by that boiling courage which was one of his most marked characteristics, determined to lead the attack in person, and placed himself in front of the left of Somerset's brigade. For the commander of the whole of the cavalry to occupy such a position was to violate the rules of the art of war, for it is evident that, as soon as the charge commenced, it would be impossible for him to exercise due control and supervision; but it was of such importance to establish from the very first the superiority of our horsemen over those of the French, that Lord Uxbridge deemed himself justified in departing from custom. At all events, it must be admitted that Lord Uxbridge's fault was one on the right side, and that his personal daring raised the enthusiasm of his followers to the highest pitch.

The French cavalry, with the utmost confidence and steadiness, notwithstanding a close fire of artillery, surmounted the ridge. The trumpets sounded, the cry of *"Vive V Empereur"* was uttered by 2,000 men, and the brilliant mass of cavalry dashed at the British squares, which, weak and few in number, were dotted about the reverse slope of the position. They had just received the fire of the British infantry, when Somerset's brigade, in beautiful order, and as enthusiastic as their opponents, dashed at full speed into the ranks of the latter.

It is seldom that two hostile ranks of cavalry meet each other at full speed, but here there was no drawing of rein, no attempt to avoid the combat. Both lines were confident in their own prowess, and resolved on victory.

The British, in obedience to the national instinct for close fighting, and because their swords were shorter than those of the Cuirassiers, seemed to a spectator to be trying to wedge themselves in between the files of the enemy, and a desperate *aula* ensued. It did not last long, however. Though our cavalry had no armour, and their swords were shorter than those of the French, their superior strength and dogged disposition soon told. The Frenchmen fought pluckily, and for a few minutes cuts and thrusts were fiercely exchanged, and the clash of arms, the ringing sound of smitten armour, oaths, shouts, and groans caused a tumult which could be heard at a considerable distance.

In the wild confusion could be seen, now a man falling heavily from his saddle, now horse and rider both sinking together,—here a steed rearing, there another dashing wildly from the crowd, in the midst of which his master was being trampled to death. Soon the blue and steely mass of Frenchmen was seen to be riven by the red-clothed troopers of England. Single Cuirassiers, breaking away from the flanks and rear, galloped wildly off, but the majority of the pride of Napoleon's cavalry kept together, and were slowly being pressed down the ascent, which a few moments before they had ascended in full confidence of victory.

This was the scene on the right and centre of Somerset's brigade. On the left, where the 2nd Life Guards were, the fight was of a different nature. The British line struck the French line somewhat obliquely, the right of the former coming first into contact with the enemy. In front of the Cuirassiers opposed to the 2nd Life Guards was a hollow way leading into the Charleroi road. The Cuirassiers were checked by this obstacle, which caused some confusion in their ranks, and scarcely had they scrambled up the opposite bank than they saw the 2nd Life Guards coming down on them at full speed, and in splendid order.

Under such circumstances, it was evident to the Frenchmen that their overthrow was inevitable, so, hastily regaining the hollow way, they filed off as rapidly as possible by their right into, and across, the Charleroi road, and took refuge amidst a cloud of French skirmishers. The 2nd Life Guards followed them hotly, but were themselves thrown into some confusion as they descended the steep bank. When the Cuirassiers found themselves on open ground and among their own people, they reined up, and, facing about, engaged in a series of hand-to-hand combats with their pursuers. They quickly discovered, however, that in this sort of fighting the British were more than their match, and soon the whole of the Cuirassiers were either slain, prisoners, prostrate on the ground, or fleeing back to the French position at top speed.

The 2nd Life Guards, having few hedges in their front, impetuously followed, passed several columns of French infantry, and penetrated to the very centre of the French first line. One troop, indeed, under Captain Kenyon, galloped along the Charleroi road up to a battery, capturing several pieces. Pressed, however, on all sides by superior numbers, they dismounted the guns, and sought to regain their ranks. This they soon did; but the regiment had, in its eagerness, advanced too far, and, attacked by a corps of Lancers treble its own strength, and fired on by the columns of French infantry, its loss was very heavy; and when it reoccupied its old position the 2nd Life Guards was sadly reduced in numbers.

In returning from the first charge, Lord Edward Somerset's horse was knocked over by a cannon-shot just as he reached a hedge a little in front of the infantry. An officer, as he galloped past, shouted to him to scramble through as quickly as possible. He did so on his hands and knees, without waiting to rise to his feet, and only just in time, for he was scarcely through the hedge when some of the enemy's cavalry rode up.

Let us see now what part Shaw took in this glorious feat of arms. It is very difficult to-ascertain precisely when his fighting came to an end. According to Siborne, Corporal Shaw, after slaying *nine* of the Cuirassiers during this charge, was killed by one of his antagonists with a carbine. We are, however, inclined to believe that this is a mistake, and that he survived to take part in several later encounters. When the regiment first came into contact with the Cuirassiers, probably at the point where the hollow way joined the Charleroi road, one of the latter awaited the onset, and seemed anxious to challenge him to single combat. Shaw was not the man to decline such an invitation, and rode straight at his opponent. The latter thrust strongly at Shaw below the belt. "Foul," we may imagine the pugilist saying to himself, as he swiftly parried. The next moment the Life Guardsman's sword cut right through the Frenchman's helmet and skull down to the chin, and to use the expression of an eye-witness, the hapless Cuirassier's "face fell off like a bit of apple." Having thus blooded his maiden sword, Shaw hastens to join his comrades, among whom are many powerful, gallant men, each deserving a separate page of history.

Two soldiers, Dakin and Hodgson by name, appear to have been friends of Shaw, and to have emulated his prowess and courage. Dakin, as he nears the foe, seems possessed with battle fury. He foams at the mouth, he shouts and curses like a maniac, but his martial rage does not interfere with his skill. While following up the retreating Cuirassiers, two of them turn on him, but with the prowess of a Paladin, Dakin, dealing two mighty blows, splits both their heads, and rides on, thirsting for further carnage. Mean time, Shaw has come up, and, seeing an eagle, slays its bearer, and is about to seize the glorious trophy, when he is obliged to relinquish it, and cut his way through the crowd of foemen clustering' round him. Hodgson, whom we have mentioned above, proves himself well worthy to be a comrade of Shaw. When the regiment is hunting the Cuirassiers off the field, Hodgson rides out in advance, and dashes singly at a French battery. Finding himself alone, he turns his horse's head, and seeks to return. A' French column intervenes. Hodgson dashes straight at it. The Frenchmen, thunderstruck by his audacity, open out to let him pass, but as soon as he is clear send a shower of bullets after him. Not one strikes him. Surely Fortune, who proverbially favours the brave, will now carry him back in safety to the British position! It would seem not, for scarcely has Hodgson heard the bullets destined for him whistle harmlessly past, than a fresh peril presents itself. A Cuirassier—Irish by birth— places himself in Hodgson's path, and shouting, " Damn you, I '11 stop your crowing," fiercely attacks the Life Guardsman. Hodgson, coolly guiding his horse with his legs, and watching his opportunity, sees it, as the Cuirassier delivers a thrust at his throat. Instead of parrying, Hodgson, with one tremendous sweep of his sword, lops off his antagonist's right hand, and then, plunging his weapon into the Cuirassier's throat, turns it round and round till the poor wretch drops heavily from his horse. Yet another proof was required of the Guardsman's prowess. Scarcely has he rid himself of the Irishman, than he is attacked by an officer of the latter's regiment. Hodgson, elated by his recent success, confidently spurs to meet his new enemy. A well-directed Llow on the nape of the neck of the Frenchman's charger brings horse and man to the ground. The officer's helmet falling off, Hodgson sees that the wearer is a greyheaded old man, and, according to his own account, would have spared him, but, perceiving a body of French Lancers approach, he considers it necessary, for his own safety, to despatch the officer, and, cutting him down, he gallops off, this time without any hindrance. This explanation is scarcely intelligible, and we can only suppose that, drunk with blood, he, under the influence of excitement, was guilty of a deed which, in his cooler moments, he would never have performed.

Another of Shaw's comrades displayed similar intrepidity, enjoyed equal good fortune. In the charge above mentioned, John Johnson, for that was his name, having outridden his comrades, saw before him three Cuirassiers. So great was already the dread of the Life Guards, that these men fled before a single antagonist. They entered a narrow lane, and Johnson unhesitatingly followed them. On coming to the end of the lane, and discovering no opening, the Frenchmen turned to bay. Without a moment's pause, Johnson dashed at them, and having, after a short conflict, disabled one or all of their number, he took all three as prisoners back to his regiment.

CHAPTER V.

E now return to Shaw himself. After the glorious charge which we have described, he returned with his regiment to their old position just in rear of the ridge. There they were drawn up in line ready to charge again should opportunity offer. When the 2nd Life Guards reformed and told off, the terrible loss which they had suffered became apparent. As for Shaw, he found that the two files which in the morning had stood right and left of him were absent. They had been slain, as his comrades told him.

For some two hours the 2nd Life Guards had to stand the severest trial to which a soldier can be exposed, *i.e.,* that of remaining inactive under a heavy cannonade, for though they could not see the enemy, his shot and shell came constantly over the ridge, and men and horses from time to time went_down before it. No unsteadiness, however, ensued. The Life Guards felt that the eyes not only of the army but of the country were upon them; that first in rank of all corps, it behoved them to show that they were inferior in courage to none, and especially that they were required to set an example to the foreign troops in Wellington's army.

Never, therefore, even on the Horse Guards Parade, had the Household Cavalry been so stolidly immovable as on that memorable Sunday when Napcleon fought his last fight for the championship of the world. Every now and then a round shot would bury itself with a squelch in the body of a horse, or with an indescribable sound reduce his rider to a bloody mass. From time to time a shrieking shell would burst in the midst of a line, the iron fragments scattering death and wounds on all sides. Occasionally, too, grape, with a hum like the sound of the flight of a covey of partridges, or a random musket bullet, with a hum, would cause a horse to plunge, rear, or stagger to the ground, or a trooper to turn suddenly pale, reel in his" saddle, and fall to the ground.

With heroic endurance, Somerset's horsemen bore themselves as if death and mutilation had nought to do with those who were untouched, and every gap in the ranks was promptly filled up.

About four o'clock the cannonade increased in fury, and it soon became evident that it was the prelude to another desperate effort to drive the British from the field. The infantry were to attack La Haye Sainte and Hougomont; but the chief blow was to be dealt by the cavalry on that part of the British position lying between those two posts. Ney, who commanded in that part of the field, formed up Milhaud's Cuirassiers, twenty-four squadrons, in first line, seven squadrons of Lancers of the Guard on the second line, and twelve squadrons of Chasseurs of the Guard on the third line. Each regiment was drawn up in column of squadrons.

As they advanced, the second and third lines obliqued somewhat to the left, so as to come on in echelon from the right.

When they began to ascend the ridge, the French artillery necessarily ceased firing, and the British guns were able to concentrate all their attention on the French cavalry, whom they plied rapidly with grape.

Notwithstanding the havoc wrought in their ranks the French came gallantly on, in good order and well in hand. At length the guns are but forty yards distant. At this moment the British artillery officers give the word "Fire," the iron hail tears through the hostile masses, laying low many a gallant horseman and his steed. Not a moment, however, do the Cuirassiers pause. On the contrary, the trumpets sound the charge, and the mail-clad squadrons make a rush at the batteries with a shout.

As they emerge from the smoke they find not a soul left to oppose them. The guns are there, still reeking from the recent discharge, and the ground is strewed with dead and wounded men; but every artilleryman able to move has, in obedience to the Duke's orders, taken refuge with the infantry in rear.

Astonished at their victory, and intoxicated with the delight of gaining possession of the whole line of batteries, the Cuirassiers raise cries of "Victoire," "Vive l'Empereur," "En avant," and, resuming their onward career, dash at speed against the infantry, whose squares, placed chequer-wise, occupy the further slope of the heights. The Lancers and Chasseurs, intoxicated by the sight, increase their pace, and soon are almost up in line with the Cuirassiers. The French cavalry charge with fury on the squares, but these latter stand firm, and, reserving their fire till the cavalry have approached to within thirty paces, then open on them with destructive effect. The leading squadron of each regiment on this opens out from the centre, and, passing by the flanks of the square, receiving their fire as they do so, make for squares further in rear. Each succeeding squadron repeated this manoeuvre. The natural result was, the whole attacking force was soon broken up into a number of confused and disorganized masses, the men of different squadrons, and even sometimes of different regiments, becoming mixed up together. Now was the opportunity for the British cavalry, and they promptly

seized it, Somerset's and the other brigades in that part of the line advancing in beautiful order, and, after a slight resistance, driving the French cavalry off from the squares, over the crest of the ridge, and down the exterior slope. The enemy's horsemen soon rallied at the foot of the height, and, furious at finding victory snatched from them when it appeared to be actually within their grasp, prepared for a renewed attack. They had been taught caution, but their enthusiasm was undiminished. This time a portion only of the French cavalry was told off to attack the squares, while the remainder were withheld to deal with the British Dragoons. The squares were,however, charged in the same manner as on the previous occasion, and with a similar result.

Gradually the first line of cavalry became exhausted by its vain efforts, but the supports were in good order, and advanced to charge our horsemen. These did not await the onslaught, but moved forward to meet it with great steadiness and determination. A murderous struggle ensued, but the French, pressed in front by the British cavalry, and suffering in flank from the re of our infantry, could not maintain their ground, and went headlong down the slope, followed by their pertinacious foe, whose grasp it was difficult to shake off.

Notwithstanding the little effect produced by the beating of those cavalry waves against such immovable rocks as the British infantry, Napoleon determined to persevere in his faulty tactics. The shattered squadrons which had twice been driven off the ridge were reinforced by Kellerman's corps, consisting of seven squadrons of Dragoons, eleven of Cuirassiers, and six of Carabiniers, and by Guyot's Heavy Cavalry of the Guard, composed of six squadrons of Horse Grenadiers and seven of Dragoons.

With this enormous mass of cavalry, making up, with the troops engaged previously, eighty squadrons, a renewed attack was made on the same portion of Wellington's position—namely, the right. Siborne, from whose trustworthy pages we have gathered many of the particulars

D above given, describes this supreme effort of the French cavalry in the following eloquent words:—

"When the tremendous cavalry force which they had thus assembled moved forward to the attack, the whole space between La Haye Sainte and Hougomont appeared one moving glittering mass, and as it approached the Anglo-allied position, undulating with the conformation of the ground, it resembled a sea in agitation. Upon reaching the crest of the ridge and regaining temporary possession of the batteries, its very shouts sounded on the distant ear like the ominous roar of breakers thundering on the shore. Like waves following in quick succession, the whole mass now appeared to roll over the ridge, and, as the light curling smoke arose from the fire which was opened by the squares, and by which the latter sought to stem the current of the advancing host, it resembled the foam and spray thrown up by the mighty waters as they dash on isolated rocks and beetling crags; and as the mass separated and rushed in every direction, completely covering the interior slope, it bore the appearance of innumerable eddies and counter-currents threatening to overwhelm and engulph the obstructions by which its onward course had been opposed. The storm continued to rage with the greatest violence, and the devoted squares seemed lost in the midst of the tumultuous onset. In vain did the maddening mass chafe and fret away its strength against those impregnable barriers, which, based upon the sacred principles of honour, discipline, and duty, and cemented by the ties of patriotism and the impulse of national glory, stood proudly unmoved and inaccessible. Disorder and confusion, produced by the commingling of corps, and by the scattering fire from the faces of the chequered squares, gradually led to the retreat of parties of horsemen across the ridge; these were followed by broken squadrons, and at length the retrograde movement became general. Then the allied Dragoons, who had been judiciously kept in readiness to act at the favourable moment, darted forward to complete the disorganization and overthrow of the now receding waves of the French cavalry."

In all these charges Shaw and his gallant comrades took part, and showed themselves to be brave amongst the brave.

One trooper of the 2nd Life Guards, named Samuel Godley, who, from being bald, was nicknamed by the regiment, "The Marquis of Granby," had his horse shot under him. As he fell his helmet tumbled off, and ere he could rise he perceived a Cuirassier hastening up to despatch him. He had scarcely struggled to his feet when the Frenchman was upon him. Notwithstanding the odds against Godley, — for he was on foot, shaken by his fall, his head was bare, and he had no defensive armour,—he succeeded in killing his antagonist, and rode off in triumph on his foeman's steed amidst the cheers of his comrades, who exclaimed, "Well done, Marquis of Granby!"

Shortly afterwards, the horse thus gallantly won, was killed by a cannonshot, and Godley was seriously injured in the head by the fall.

Godley was discharged in 1824, and died in 1831. His comrades placed a headstone to his grave, with an appropriate inscription, in St. John's Wood Chapel.

To resume our narrative. The French cavalry had scarcely disappeared, and the British artillery had only been able to send a few shots after them, when their supports renewed the attack on the infantry squares. Again we extract from Siborne's book a passage which gives a brilliant description of a scene which, in splendour and interest, has never been surpassed in war:—

"Failing in their direct attack, they rode through the intervals between the squares in all directions, exhibiting extraordinary coolness and intrepidity. Some of the most daring approached close up to the ranks to draw forth the fire from a square, and thus secure a better chance of success for the squadron, prepared to seize the advantage, and to charge. Small parties of desperate fellows would endeavour to force an opening at some weak point by cutting aside the bayonets, and firing at the defenders with their pistols. But the squares were proof against every assault and every stratagem. More cavalry crossed over the summit of the ridge; and the greater part of the interior slope occupied by the allied right wing seemed covered with horsemen of all kinds—Cuirassiers, Lancers, Carabineers, Chasseurs, Dragoons, and Horse Grenadiers.

"The French, enraged at their want of success, brandishing their swords, and exciting one another by cries of 'Vive PEmpereur,' reiterated their attacks with redoubled and fruitless vigour.

"Like the majestic oaks of the forest, which are poetically said to strike their roots deeper and more tenaciously into the earth as the fury of the storm increases, so stood the Anglo-allied squares, grand in the imposing attitude of their strength, and bidding defiance to the tempestuous elements by which they were assailed on every side.

"At length the attack evinced symptoms of exhaustion; the charges became less frequent and less vigorous; disorder and confusion were rapidly augmenting; the spirit of enthusiasm and the confidence of superiority were quickly yielding to the feeling of despondence and the sense of hopelessness.

"The Anglo-allied cavalry again advanced, and once more swept the mingled host—comprising every description of mounted troops — from off the ground on which they had so fruitlessly frittered away their strength."

It was in this charge—the last but one made by the 2nd Life Guards—that the gallant Shaw struck his last blow. He had been foremost among his brave comrades the whole day, and is said to have slain a fabulous number of Frenchmen, receiving, however, numerous sword-cuts in the course of the fight.

When the British cavalry swept away, as Siborne has described, the remains of the French horsemen, who, unsupported by infantry, had so persistently and vainly striven to break the British squares, Shaw still rode with his comrades. In the *milee* he found himself isolated, and surrounded by *ten* of the enemy's horsemen. Whirling his good blade swiftly around, he for a time keeps his foes at bay. At length his sword breaks in his hand; but Shaw will not give in. Hurling the hilt of his now useless weapon from him, he tears his helmet from his head, and tries to use it as a cestus. The Cuirassiers now close in upon him, and the heroic Guardsman is struck to the earth, and they ride off exulting in the thought that they have at length avenged the hecatomb of Frenchmen who have fallen victims to Shaw's slaughtering right hand.

Here we for a time lose sight of our hero; indeed, there are many accounts of the manner in which he lost his life. The one we have given, however, we believe to be correct.

It would appear that after being cut down, Shaw, who had been repeatedly wounded during the day, and had lost much blood, was still able to crawl, and with, as we may imagine, great difficulty and suffering made his way slowly to the front. Either he was dazed by his injuries, or he was unable to move till the battle had been won, when he instinctively staggered on in the track of the victors.

That he must have proceeded towards Charleroi instead of Waterloo is evident from the following circumstance: A wounded comrade, after being dragged by the French some distance to their rear, was, in the panic which ensued, allowed to sink down on a dunghill near an inn in one of the villages on the Charleroi road, and there he met Shaw. This village must have been La Belle Alliance, for we can hardly imagine that two desperately wounded men, however far in advance they had fallen, could have proceeded further. At all events, according to Kelly's 'Battle of Waterloo,' the released Life Guardsman was aroused from the stupor into which he had fallen, by some one creeping to his side. He feebly turned his head, and beheld Shaw almost cut to pieces, and scarcely able to move, endeavouring to approach him.

On recognizing a well-known face, Shaw faintly whispered,—" Ah, my dear fellow, I'm done for."

A few words passed between them, but neither was able to say much, and the Life Guardsman who related the story said that he soon fell into the sleep of exhaustion. In the morning he awoke, and found Shaw " lying dead, with his face leaning on his hand, as if he had breathed his last while in a state of insensibility His death was occasioned rather by the loss of blood from a variety of wounds than the magnitude of any one."

Thus perished, in the prime of life and the fulness of vigour, one of the most gallant and formidable troopers who ever rode with England's squadrons to battle, and it is meet that his fame should be perpetuated by the statue too tardily erected to his memory.

CHAPTER VI.

E must now return to the 2nd Life Guards, and see how they played out their part in the great struggle. Soon after Shaw's disappearance, too late, Napoleon and Ney recognized the fact that cavalry, aided only by artillery, could not force the British position. A change in the enemy's tactics took place, and a strong column of infantry, supported by cavalry, advanced against the centre of Wellington's right wing.

To ward off the blow, Lord Uxbridge ordered up Somerset's brigade. They charged with unabated gallantry, and checked the enemy's advance; but, being much reduced in numbers, they were unable to penetrate the infantry column, and were ordered to retire.

From this time to the end of the battle Somerset's brigade remained in support on the reverse slope of the ridge. They had not long been there—still suffering much loss from the enemy's artillery fire—when La Haye Sainte was captured, the French infantry gained the summit of the ridge in the rear, the troops which occupied that position were being gradually pressed back, and Wellington's centre seemed on the point of being forced.

Fortunately, the arrival of the great Duke in person, and of Vivian's Hussar brigade, brought in haste from the extreme left, averted the catastrophe; but

for a few minutes the fate of the day trembled in the balance.

When Vivian's Hussars came up, their leader, seeing Lord Edward Somerset, rode up, and said, "Where is your brigade?"

"Here," was the reply of Lord Edward, pointing, firstly, to a small band of horsemen amounting to »little more than a squadron, and then to the ground covered with dead and dying, clad in red, and with mutilated horses, wandering or turning in circles, he displayed to him the wreck of what had once been the Household and Union Brigades of cavalry combined—a force amounting, at the commencement of the action, to upwards of 2,000 dragoons.

At length the Emperor shot his last bolt, and Wellington, perceiving that the French were disorganized, and that Blucher was pressing heavily on their right, ordered a:general advance, and the victory was won.

We presume that Somerset's brigade followed up the French as far as La Belle Alliance, for we know that the Union Brigade, alongside of which it had been drawn up during the latter part of the day, did so.

When the general advance was made, the late Colonel the Hon. George Damer, then a young officer on the staff,-was sent to desire Ponsonby's Union Brigade to conform to the movement. After a long search, he at last discovered them. They were reduced to a skeleton; many of the men were wounded, and the horses, panting and blown, looked completely done up. Sir William Ponsonby having been killed, the brigade was commanded by Colonel Muter, of the Inniskillings. This grave old Scotchman presented a sorry appearance, his helmet having been beaten in, and his arm being in a sling.

On receiving the order, Muter made no remark, but, with a sardonic look, got his men into a laboured canter, and, guided by Damer, led them against a body of infantry, who still stood despairingly at bay. Muter, without hesitation, shouted " Charge." As he did so, the Frenchmen fired, one of their bullets striking Damer on the knee, who, as he received the wound, heard the Colonel grumble out, as he dashed among the French,—" I think you ha' it noo, sir."

Captain Gronow, to whom we are indebted for this anecdote, in another place incidentally mentions Shaw. In the first charge of Somerset's brigade, Captain Kelly, of the 1st Life Guards, with many of his men, allowed themselves to be carried by their ardour almost up to the summit of the position occupied by the French. Saluted by a heavy fire of artillery, and attacked by fresh bodies of cavalry, the gallant band was forced to retreat. Whilst cutting their way back, they perceived Kelly cleaving his way through a host of foemen. In this strait, Shaw hastened to the side of Captain Kelly, and the *two, cutting down their antagonists as if the latter had been poppies,* regained their lines.

Of Captain Kelly it is related, that on this or another occasion, he was fiercely attacked by a Cuirassier; but though opposed to a man whose armour gave him an enormous advantage, Kelly not only successfully defended himself, but selecting, with admirable coolness, a vulnerable part of his opponent, slew him with a thrust in the neck.

CHAPTER VII. UMEROUS, indeed, were the feats of individual heroism on that glorious 18th of June, and no troops bore themselves more gallantly than the Union Brigade.

When Somerset's horsemen executed their first charge against the French cavalry, Ponsonby's brigade, posted on their left, was hurled at the infantry columns, which had already topped the summit of the ridge. The Scots Greys, on the left of the line, passed the 92nd Highlanders just as the latter regiment were charging, and the two corps were for an instant blended in one body. Fired with enthusiasm at seeing their countrymen, the Greys and Highlanders raised a terrific shout of "Scotland for ever!" So excited were the Highlanders, that many of them clung to the stirrups of the Greys, and with them plunged headlong into the hostile mass in their front, gathering impetus as they rushed down the slope.

The Frenchmen resisted bravely, but the shock was too much for them, and many a gallant soldier went down, either crushed by "those terrible grey horses," as Napoleon called them, laid low by the irresistible swords of their riders, or bayoneted by the furious and nimble Highlanders mingled with the Dragoons.

In the midst of the *milie,* Sergeant Ewart, of the Greys, saw the eagle of the French 45th of the line, a regiment which had covered itself with glory in a score of battles, and had earned for itself the title of "The Invincibles."

A devoted band rallied round the symbol of regimental honour, and prepared to die in its defence. Die most of them did, but fruitlessly; for Ewart, after a desperate struggle, carved a path to the eagle, slew the bearer of the latter after a fierce hand-to-hand fight, and carried off the cherished trophy in triumph. It is gratifying to learn that in the following year Sergeant Ewart was rewarded with a commission.

The Greys, after riving the above-mentioned column, tore wildly on without pausing an instant to reform, and made straight for a regiment in support. The outer files opened a destructive fire; but the Greys, charging down hill, had gathered such way that they could not, if they had wished, have pulled up. No thought of tightening rein, however, occurred to these gallant horsemen, and they plunged into the column of infantry in their front with irresistible force. The foremost ranks were hurled back on those in the rear, or fell to the earth to be crushed by the torrent of rushing horsemen. For a moment the mass was convulsed, and then broke up, hundreds of prisoners being secured, and the ground being strewed with dead and wounded men.

Equal destruction had been dealt by the Royal Dragoons and the Inniskillings. The Royals came upon a column of the 105th Regiment, which had just pushed through a hedge. Seized with a panic, those in front sought to recross the hedge, but were stopped by those in the rear, who were unable to see the danger. Whilst the struggle was go-

ing on, the Royals dashed into the column, slew or captured many, and sent the remainder headlong and in confusion down the slope. The officer who carried the eagle of the 105th rushed for refuge into the ranks of the 28th French regiment, which was coming up as a support. He was accompanied by a few resolute men, who constituted themselves the colour guard. Captain Clark, seeing this group, promptly cried, " Right shoulders forward; attack the colours." He himself rode straight at the eagle, and ran its bearer through the body. The eagle dropped from the hapless officer's hand and fell across the head of Captain Clark's horse. Captain Clark snatched at it, but only touched the fringe. Fortunately Corporal Stiles at the moment came up, and caught the standard ere it reached the ground. The 28th Regiment, thrown into disorder by the fugitives of the 105th, and falling fast before the swords of our Dragoons, soon broke up and fled, pursued to the foot of the ridge by the exultant Royals.

The Inniskillings disposed of the 54th and 55th Regiments in like manner, and displayed as much prowess as the remainder of the brigade.

CHAPTER VIII. ITHERTO we have spoken only of the heavies, but the light cavalry won their full share of glory, especially at the close of the day. When the final advance took place, a squadron of the ioth Hussars, commanded by Major the Honourable Frederick Howard, was ordered by General Vivian to charge a square of Grenadiers of the Guard, which, in the midst of the almost universal panic, preserved a bold attitude. Vivian himself joined in the charge, posting himself on the right of the squadron. As might have been expected, the Hussars, though they charged right up to the bayonets, were unsuccessful. Major Howard fell senseless from a shot in the mouth, and a Grenadier, stepping forward, brutally beat out his brains. Lieut. Gunning had been killed a moment previously, and two other lieutenants were wounded. Furious at their failure, and excited by the loss which they had suffered, the Hussars disdained retreat, and, though their ranks were being rapidly thinned, strove to force their way into the square. For some minutes the contest lasted, the Hussars cutting at the infantry, the latter thrusting with their bayonets, and every instant emptying a saddle with a musket-shot. Disheartened, probably, by the defeat of the French army, the Grenadiers at length yielded to the pressure of the Hussars, and gradually fell back till they reached a hollow way, into which they descended in confusion, and then broke up.

Of all the wonderful escapes at the Battle of Waterloo, the most wonderful was that of Lieut.-Colonel the Hon. F. C. Ponsonby, of the 12th Light Dragoons. That officer, leading his regiment to protect the retreat of the heavies on the first cavalry charge, first broke through an infantry column, and then smote, with untiring vigour, the flank of a body of Lancers.

The ardour of the regiment, much broken by its very successes, caused it to proceed too far, and Ponsonby was endeavouring to withdraw his men, when he was disabled in both arms by two successive blows from sabres. Losing all control over his horse, he was carried up to the crest of the French position, when a third sabre-cut struck him to the earth senseless, and apparently dead.

After a time he regained his senses, and raised his head to look about him. A Lancer, passing by, observed the movement, and, exclaiming, "Ah! rascal, you are not dead, rascal!" stabbed him in the back. Soon after, a French infantry-man came up, and plundered him.

A French officer brought up some troops to the spot where Ponsonby was lying. Perceiving the Colonel's hapless plight, he humanely ordered a knapsack to be placed under his head, and gave him a draught of brandy. Later on, a French skirmisher came up, and took advantage of the body of the English officer to obtain cover. Whilst loading, he conversed gaily with Ponsonby, telling him that the English would certainly be beaten by the Emperor. At length, however, he changed his tone, and, with a whimsical smile, observed, "Ah, in-deed, I think you English will beat the Emperor. Good-morning, my friend," and retired.

When the final advance took place, two squadrons of Prussian cavalry passed at full trot over Ponsonby, causing him much suffering.

When the action was over, a straggler belonging to the 40th Regiment, came to where Ponsonby was lying. The Colonel had by this time recovered his voice, and asked the man to remain with him till morning. He consented to do so, and when the sun rose he brought a party of the 12th Light Dragoons, who carried their commander to the rear. Wonderful to relate, Colonel Ponsonby in time entirely recovered from his desperate injuries.

The most interesting part of the story is to follow. Some years afterwards, when Colonel Ponsonby had become a General Officer, and Governor of Malta, a Baron de Laussat arrived on the island on his return from a journey in the East. He was introduced to the Governor, and, finding that the Frenchman had fought at Waterloo, Sir Frederick Ponsonby had a long conversation with him, among other things relating his own wonderful escape, and the kindness he had received from a French officer. M. de Laussat said,—" Was he not in such-and-such a uniform?" "He was," replied the General. "Did he not say so-and-so to you, and was not the cloak of such-and-such a colour?" "It was. I remember it perfectly," was the answer. Further explanation ensued, and Sir Frederick became convinced that the man to whom he had always said that he owed his life stood before him.

The characteristic of the Battle of Waterloo was that all three arms played an equal part, and the exploits of the infantry and artillery fully equalled those of the cavalry. Indeed, at Quatre Bras, which may be considered the prologue to the severer struggle of the 18th of June, there were no British cavalry on the ground.

One of the most sensational incidents of the campaign has been commemorated by a well-known print. Either at Quatre Bras or Waterloo—we cannot say which, for Cannon's record of the services of the 92nd Highlanders makes no mention of the fact—the regiment was compelled by overwhelming numbers to fall back. A gallant sergeant, perceiving that the ensign carrying one of the colours had fallen, rushed back to bring off the standard. The death-grasp of the young officer was, however, so firm that the sergeant could not disengage the colour from his hand. It was an anxious moment. The French were advancing, pouring in a shower of bullets, and were already within a few yards of the sergeant. To stay another moment was to ensure the loss of the colour and his own death or captivity. With a mighty effort, therefore, he raised the dead officer, still holding the precious emblem in his hand, and bore both back to his regiment. To the credit of the French officers, they restrained their men from firing on the heroic sergeant, and made no attempt to prevent him from rejoining his comrades. We believe that this incident occurred at Quatre Bras towards the close of the day.

Numerous other instances of individual and collective valour took place on both the 16th and 18th of June. On the former day the 42nd and 44th were in line, when they were suddenly charged from the rear by a body of Lancers, who, as they passed, had been unaccountably taken for allied cavalry. The 42nd, on discovering their mistake, hastily formed square, but the two flank companies had not yet formed the rear face when some of the Lancers came up at full gallop, drove before them several men of the two companies in question, and penetrated into the square.

The fate of any other than British infantry would have been sealed, but the Highlanders proved equal to their ancient renown. They promptly recovered from their momentary confusion, and with unparalleled courage and discipline they completed the interrupted movement, hemmed in the leading Lancers, who were either bayoneted or captured, and calmly repulsed all the efforts of the French cavalry to follow their comrades. Yet this feat was accomplished under disturbing circumstances, for the Colonel, Sir Robert Macara, was slain by a lance thrust, and within a few minutes the command of the regiment devolved upon three officers in succession.

Equally magnificent was the behaviour of the 44th. Their commander, Colonel Hamerton, seeing the Lancers swooping down on his rear, rapidly decided that there would be no time to form square. Coolly, therefore, as on parade, he gave the command, "Rear rank, right about face. Make ready," then, pausing till the Lancers were almost upon the regiment, "Present—fire." The effect of the volley, delivered with the utmost deliberation, and at only a few yards' distance, was deadly. Still, some of the bravest of the Lancers were not to be denied, and made a dash at the colours. One gallant fellow pierced Ensign Christie, who carried one of the-colours, through the left eye, the weapon penetrating to the lower jaw. The Frenchman then made an attempt to seize the prize, but Christie, notwithstanding the intolerable agony of his wound, flung himself on the colour. As the latter fell, the Frenchman carried off a piece of it on the point of his lance, but the next instant he was both shot and bayoneted by the nearest men of the 44th.

The 69th were on that day less successful than the 44th. The former regiment was in the act of deploying, when a strong body of French Cuirassiers, which, owing to the 69th being in a hollow and surrounded by high corn, had approached unperceived, charged perpendicularly on a flank, rolling up the line from one end to the other. In the confusion one of the colours was captured, notwithstanding the heroic resistance of Major Lindsay, Lieutenant Pigot, and Volunteer Clarke, who were all desperately wounded; Volunteer Clarke received no fewer than twenty-three wounds. In the course of the 16th the 69th lost more than a quarter of its strength.

On the 18th the regimental colour of the 32nd was seized, but never in danger. During the great charge of Picton's division the Ensign—Birtwhistle—car-rying the regimental colour of the 32nd was severely wounded. Lieutenant Belcher, who commanded the left centre subdivision, took the colour from him. The next moment a French cavalry officer, whose horse had been shot under him, made a snatch at it, and a struggle between him and Belcher took place. The latter strove to draw his sword, when a sergeant thrust his halbert into the Frenchman's breast, and at the same time a private shot him. Major Toole shouted, "Save the brave fellow," but the words were uttered too late.

CHAPTER IX. URING the bloody 18th of June, 1815, the endurance of the British infantry was even more remarkable than their courage. Spending hours in alternately forming square to receive the French cavalry, and lying down in line-underafearful cannonade, their loss was awful, and the test was one which no other troops could have borne. Captain Gronow, formerly of the Grenadier Guards, gives some life-like descriptions of what came under his immediate notice. "During the battle," he says, "our squares presented a shocking sight. Inside we were nearly suffocated by the smoke and smell from burnt cartridges. It was impossible to move a yard without treading upon a wounded comrade, or upon the bodies of the dead, and the loud groans of the wounded and dying were appalling. At four o'clock our square was a perfect hospital, being full of dead, dying, and mutilated soldiers. The charges of cavalry were in appearance very formidable, but, in reality, a great relief, as the artillery could no longer fire on us. The very earth shook under the enormous mass of men and horses. I shall never forget the strange noise our bullets made against the breast-plates of Kellermann's and Milhaud's Cuirassiers, six or seven thousand in number, who attacked us with great fury. I can only compare it, with a somewhat homely simile, to the noise of a violent hailstorm beating upon panes of glass. The artillery did great execution, but our musketry did not at first seem to kill many men, though it brought down a large number of horses, and created indescribable confusion.

The horses of the first rank of Cuirassiers, in spite of all the efforts of their riders, came to a standstill, shaking and covered with foam, at about twenty yards' distance from our squares, and generally resisted all attempts to charge the line of serried steel. On one occasion, two gallant French officers forced their way into a gap momentarily created by the discharge of artillery; one was killed by Staples, the other by Adair. Nothing could be more gallant than the behaviour of these veterans, many of whom had distinguished themselves on half the battle-fields of Europe. In the midst of our terrible fire, their officers were seen, as if on parade, keeping order in their ranks, and encouraging them. Unable to renew the charge, but unwilling to retreat, they brandished their swords with loud cries of ' Vive 1' Empereur,' and allowed themselves to be mowed down by hundreds rather than yield. Our men, who shot them down, could not help admiring the gallant bearing and heroic resignation of their enemies."

The courage of the French cavalry, especially the Cuirassiers, has never been surpassed. They would often ride coolly round a square, seeking for an opening. Some of them would discharge their pistols in the faces of the infantry, in order to draw their fire, and give a chance for a rush. Others actually cut at the kneeling ranks with their long swords.

A noble example of devotion was set by a Cuirassier officer. Whenever the cavalry charged, the British artillerymen, in obedience to orders, sought refuge in the nearest square. As soon as the horsemen retired, the gunners would rush out and ply the retreating foe with showers of grape. The officer in question, noticing this fact, the next time his men receded, baffled from a charge, took up his post by a gun and brandished his sword, as if defying the British to come on. He was instantly shot, but by this self-sacrifice he saved the lives of many of his comrades.

A Cuirassier fell wounded a few yards from a square of Highlanders. One of the latter rushed out to bayonet the fallen foe; but he did not blench, and quietly retaining a sitting posture, shrugged his shoulders, extended his hands in a deprecatory manner, and, in a calm, good-humoured tone, and with a smile of remonstrance, exclaimed, "Ah, Monsieur Anglais." The Gael could not resist the appeal, and, withholding his thrust, said, "Go to the rear, you—" an order which the Frenchman was not slow to obey.

Lieutenant-Colonel Colquitt, of the Grenadier Guards, was inside a square, formed by his battalion, and, like every one else, lying down in order to diminish the effect of a severe artillery fire. Suddenly a shell alighted at his side. Without an instant's hesitation, he raised the missile, and, by a vigorous effort, threw it over the heads of the men, and down a declivity in front before it burst.

A sergeant of the same regiment, at the crisis of the battle, fearing that his battalion, suffering from a heavy fire of grape, and threatened by a French regiment of Infantry, would give way, bethought him of the following means of encouraging his comrades. Ensign Pardoe had been killed, and during a temporary retreat of the battalion, his corpse had been stripped by the French, who, however, had left on the ground his blood-stained coat. The sergeant in question, whose name, we regret to say has not been recorded, stepped out of the ranks, and, picking up the ensign's coat, waved it like a banner, saying, "When our officers bleed, we should not reckon our lives dear." This action he repeated, when the Imperial Guards attacked, and, to quote his own modest words, "I believe it had its desired effect. I thought," said the sergeant, in a private letter, "if anything would stimulate the men, this would be effective. An officer, having just sacrificed his life for his country's safety, ours were pledged for the same. The men fought with all their might, and, in half an hour, as I mentioned, we cut the 105th Regiment to pieces, and took one stand of colours. Had I known, however, that the coat would have been mentioned farther than to my wife, I should not have inserted it, but let that fact have been mentioned by

others, as I do not like to commend myself."

It is asserted that the Duke of Wellington, when the final attack was made on the British centre, called out, "Up, Guards, and at them!" and that when subsequently some of the Imperial Guard were summoned to surrender, General Cambronne said, "La Garde meurt et ne se rend pas."

Captain Gronow, who stood close to Wellington when he ordered the charge, and subsequently spent many years in Paris, is a good authority on these points. He says, "It was at this moment that the Duke of Wellington gave his famous order for our bayonet charge, as he rode along the line; these are the precise words he made use of, 'Guards, get up and charge.' We were instantly on our legs. They had been lying down previously, and, after so many hours of inaction and irritation at maintaining a purely defensive attitude, all the time suffering the loss of comrades and friends, the spirit which animated officers and men may be easily imagined. After firing a volley, as soon as the enemy were within shot, we rushed on with fixed bayonets and that hearty hurrah peculiar to British soldiers. It appeared that our men, deliberately, and with calculation, singled out their victims, for, as they came upon the Imperial Guard, our line broke, and the fighting became irregular. The impetuosity of our men seemed almost to paralyze their enemies. I witnessed several of the Imperial Guard, who were run through the body, apparently without any resistance on their parts. I observed a big Welshman, of the name of Hughes, who was six feet seven inches in height, run through with his bayonet and knock down with the butt end of his firelock, I should think a dozen, at least, of his opponents. This terrible contest did not last more than ten minutes, for the Imperial Guard was soon in full retreat, leaving all their guns and many prisoners in our hands. The famous General Cambronne was taken prisoner, fighting hand to hand with the gallant Sir Colin Halkett, who was shortly after shot through the cheek by a grape shot. Cambronne's supposed

answer,' La Garde ne Sq rend pas,' was an invention of after times, and he himself always denied having used such an expression."

Siborne relates that when, in 1844, it was proposed to erect at Nantes a monument to the memory of Cambronne, and to inscribe the words in question on the pedestal, the family of General Michel, who was killed in the last attack on the British position, protested that it was Michel, not Cambronne, who said, "La Garde meurt," &c. As a matter of fact, many of the Garde Imperiale *did* surrender.

Nothing could have been finer than the conduct of the British Guards, both those who defended Hougomont, and those who fought on the ridge. Among the most gallant of the former was Sergeant Graham, of the Coldstreams. The French, advancing in superior numbers, followed the British so closely in their retreat into the great court-yard, that the latter were unable to close the gate. The British then took refuge behind the nearest cover, and after a short, sharp fusillade, charged. A desperate struggle ensued, but at length Lieutenant-Colonel Macdonnell, Captain Wyndham, Ensigns Gooch and Hervey, and Sergeant Graham succeeded in closing the gate.

A little later, when the contest was most severe, and the result doubtful, Sergeant Graham asked Lieutenant-Colonel Macdonnell's permission to fall out. Surprised at such a request from a soldier of approved gallantry at a moment when every man was wanted, he asked Graham why he wanted to leave the ranks. The Sergeant explained that he wished to save his brother, then lying wounded in a burning out-house, and that, having accomplished this task, he would return. Leave was granted, and Graham, having carried his brother to a place of safety, fell in again as he had promised.

A few months later, a patriotic clergyman—the Rev. Mr. Norcott, of Framlingham, Suffolk, wrote to the Duke of Wellington, expressing a wish to bestow an annuity of ten pounds on some Waterloo soldier, to be named by his

Grace. Sergeant Graham was the person selected; but, unfortunately for him, Mr. Norcott became bankrupt at the end of two years, and the annuity ceased.

The following quaint story is told of a certain Major of the 42nd Highlanders, who must have been Major Menzies. On his choosing to fight on foot, he had given his horse to a drummer. After being repeatedly wounded the Major fell exhausted from loss of blood, near a private named Donald M'Intosh, who received a mortal wound at the same time. The drummer quitted the horse to assist Donald, and a French Lancer passing by made a dash at the animal. M'Intosh on this called out, "Hoot, mon, ye mauna tak that beast. She belangs to our Major here." The Lancer paying no heed to this remonstrance, Donald levelled his musket, shot the man dead, and then fell back a corpse.

Immediately afterwards an officer of Cuirassiers rode up, and, perceiving that the Major was alive, stooped to despatch him with his sword. The wounded man was not one tamely to accept his fate, and, seizing his wouldbe murderer by the leg, dragged him from the saddle. A Lancer came up to assist the Frenchman, but Major Menzies, by a violent jerk, placed the Cuirassier officer above, and the lance entered the wrong man just below the cuirass.

For some ten minutes the Major lay helpless, with his dying foe upon him. At the end of that time the Frenchman rose with difficulty to his feet, staggered a few paces, and then dropped down dead. It is satisfactory to be able to add that the Major eventually recovered, and lived many years, bearing upon his body the scars of no fewer than sixteen wounds received at Quatre Bras, besides one of a severe hurt inflicted at Badajos.

Three companies of the Rifle Brigade were posted in a sand-pit to the left of La Haye Sainte. The French attacked them in force, and one of their officers came to the front of his men, and challenged, by his gestures, any Englishman to single combat. A gigantic Highlander, 6 feet 6 inches in height, strode forward to meet him, and a duel ensued,

both sides suspending fighting for a moment to look at it. The contest was soon ended. The Frenchman made a thrust at his adversary's body, but missed the latter, and pierced his arm instead. The Highlander, enraged at the wound, brought down his Regulation sword—a trumpery half-moon sabre—on his opponent's head. The blow, delivered with tremendous force, fell on the Frenchman's shako, which saved its wearer from a cloven skull. The sword broke off close to the hilt, and the Highlander was apparently at the mercy of his foe. Not so, however, for the stalwart rifleman dashed his fist, with the hilt and the broken blade, straight at the face of the Frenchman, who fell dead.

In the same regiment, *i.e.* the 95th, now the Rifle Brigade, an officer received a wound, which had a very remarkable result. At the storming of Badajos, in 1812, a musket-ball entered his right ear, and came out at the back of his neck. After a painful illness he recovered, but his head got a twist, and he always seemed as if he were looking over his right shoulder. At the battle of Waterloo, he was struck by another bullet, which entered the left ear, came out at the back of the neck, within half-an-inch of the point of exit of the first bullet, and set his head straight again. The name of this officer was Worsley.

Sir John Kincaid, from whose 'Random Shots of a Rifleman' we have extracted the two previous anecdotes, tells a story of the wonderful self-possession of an officer under fire. Sir John Lambert, commanding a brigade, was heard, in the midst of a terrific storm of shot, to call one of his commanding-officers to order, for repeating his (the General's) word of command, telling him that, as the regiments were in contiguous columns, they ought to take it from himself.

We have not hitherto spoken of the Artillery, yet they, as usual, behaved nobly on that bloody day. Greatly overmatched by the enemy's guns, they, nevertheless, maintained the terrible duel with dogged courage, and contributed much to the success of the day. When charged by the French cavalry, they

fired till the last moment, and then took refuge in the nearest square. On the retreat of the cavalry, they never failed to rush back to their guns, and to send showers of grape after the receding foe. One troop, commanded by Captain Mercer, suffered so terribly in horses and men, that, at the end of the day, it was literally unable to move. Its position could be recognized from the opposite ridge by the dark patch composed of dead horses and men.

Shortly before Donzelôt's attack on La Haye Sainte, Sergeant Daniel Dermot found himself, owing to the wound of his officer, in command of a rocket-party. " The Sergeant," says Siborne, "on perceiving the advance of the nearest French column towards the farm, dismounted his men, as coolly and deliberately as if exercising on Woolwich Common, though without any support whatever; laid rockets on the ground, and discharged them in succession into the mass, every one of them appearing to take effect. The advance of the column was checked, and was not resumed until Sergeant Dermot, having expended all his rockets, retired with his party, to rejoin the guns in rear."

The German Legion, many officers and men of which had graduated in the Duke of Wellington's practical war school in the Peninsula, proved themselves at Waterloo well worthy to fight in the ranks of the British army. They particularly distinguished themselves by the defence of La Haye Sainte, which, though less successful, was no less gallant than that of Hougomont.

Siborne tells us that " one of the men, named Frederick Linden, bleeding from two wounds in his head, and carrying in his pocket a large bag full of gold which he had taken from a French officer, stood at the small barn-door facing the yard, defending from thence the open western entrance. Major Baring observing that the cloth bound round his head did not suffice to stop the strong flow of blood, called out to him to withdraw; but the latter, as heedless of his wounds as of his gold, replied,—' None but a scoundrel would desert you as long as his head remains upon his shoulders!' This brave fellow was afterwards taken prisoner, and lost his treasure."

At length Baring, finding the ammunition of his men exhausted, and that they were being picked off by the enemy without the means of reta%tion, resolved to evacuate his post. In the face of the numbers of Frenchmen who were pressing on, the retreat was very difficult, and many of the Legion were cruelly massacred by the French, who seemed on that day to be destitute of all feelings of humanity. The following is extracted from Siborne:—

"The passage through the farm-house to the garden in the rear was narrow, and here the officers endeavoured to halt the men, and make one more charge; but as the French had already commenced firing down the passage, this was found impracticable.

"Ensign Frank, on perceiving a French soldier levelling his musket at Lieutenant Groeme, called out to the latter to take care; but as he was still trying to rally his men, he replied,—' Never mind, let the rascal fire!' At this instant the piece was levelled, but it fell to the ground with its owner, whom Ensign Frank had stabbed in time to save his friend.

"The French were now rushing into the house, and the foremost of them having fired at Ensign Frank, his arm was shattered by the bullet. Nevertheless, he contrived to obtain shelter in a bed-chamber, and succeeded in concealing himself under the bed. Two of the men also took refuge in the same room; but the French followed close at their heels, crying,—' Pas de pardon ces coquins verds!' and shot them dead close to Ensign Frank, who had the merited good fortune of remaining undiscovered, until the house again fell into the hands of the Allies.

Lieutenant Groeme, who had continued in the passage, was suddenly seized by the collar by a French officer, who exclaimed to his men,—' C'est ce coquin!' Their bayonets were immediately thrust at him, but he managed to parry them with his sword; and as the officer for a moment relinquished his grasp, Groeme darted along the passage, theFrench firing two shots at him, and calling out,— 'Coquin!' but they did not follow him, and he succeeded in rejoining the remnant of his battalion."

CHAPTER X.

MONG the officers who fell at Waterloo, no one was more regretted by the nation and the army than Sir Thomas Picton. Somewhat harsh and stern in his public capacity, he was, in private life, kind, humane, benevolent and charitable. He never attained to a higher command than that of a division, and a certain rashness and impracticability of temper, perhaps, unfitted him for higher functions.

As a leader on the field of battle, however, he was unequalled. He received his orders to join the Army in Belgium somewhat late, which is a fact not creditable to the authorities at the Horse Guards—the Duke himself was little consulted as to the composition of his staff—and did not leave London till the i ith of June.

He had apparently a presentiment that he was about to fight his last fight. He made his will before leaving home, and told a friend that he did not expect to return, but that when his friend heard of his death, he would hear of a bloody day. A week later he received, while cheering on his men to the charge, a bullet in the forehead, and fell dead from his horse.

Captain Gronow, who accompanied him from England, and rode on his staff at Quatre Bras, speaks of him thus:—

" Sir Thomas Picton was a stern-looking, strongbuilt man, about the middle height, and considered very like the Hetman, Platoff. He generally wore a blue frock-coat, very tightly buttoned up to the throat; a very large black silk neckcloth, showing little or no shirtcollar; dark trousers, boots, and a round hat: it was in this very dress that he was attired at Quatre Bras, as he had hurried off to the scene of action before his uniform arrived."

On the morning of his arrival at Brussels, while breakfasting with his staff, he was informed that the Duke of Wellington wished to see him immediately. Gronow thus describes the meeting:—"Sir Thomas lost not a moment in obeying the order of his chief, leaving the breakfast-table and proceeding to the park, where Wellington was walking with Fitzroy Somerset and the Duke of Richmond. Picton's manner was always more familiar than the Duke liked in his lieutenants, and on this occasion he approached him in a careless sort of way, just as he might have met an equal. The Duke bowed coldly to him, and said,—' I am glad you are come, Sir Thomas; the sooner you get on horseback the better; no time is to be lost. You will take the command of the troops in advance. The Prince of Orange knows by this time that you will go to his assistance.' Picton appeared not to like the Duke's manner; for, when he bowed and left, he muttered a few words, which convinced those who were with him that he was not much pleased with his interview."

It was not generally known till after his death, that Picton had received a painful wound at Quatre Bras, which fact he had kept secret in order that he might not be prevented from taking part in the great battle which every one expected. When, however, his corpse was laid out, it appeared, to quote Siborne, that the skin on one side, just above the hip, was raised into a very large bladder, and distended with a mass of coagulated blood, unaccompanied by any abrasion. It was supposed that the injury was caused by the wind of a round shot, and it was evident that it had been inflicted before the 18th. Whether Picton's Staff knew of his wound we cannot say, but Gronow says that when passing the General's room on the evening of the 17th, on his way to sup with one of the latter's Aides-de-Camp, he heard Sir Thomas groaning.

About 4 P.m., when the French cavalry were sweeping over the British ridge like successive waves, the Duke of Wellington took refuge in the square formed by Captain Gronow's battalion. The Duke was "accompanied only by one Aide-de-Camp; all the rest of his Staff being either killed or wounded. Our Commander-in-Chief, as far as I could judge, appeared perfectly composed; but looked very thoughtful and pale. He was dressed in a grey great coat with a cape, white cravat, leather pantaloons, Hessian boots, and a large cocked hat, *a la Russe.* . The Duke sat unmoved, mounted on his favourite charger. I recollect his asking Colonel Stanhope what o'clock it was, upon which Stanhope took out his watch, and said it was twenty minutes past four. The Duke replied, 'The battle is mine; and if the Prussians arrive soon, there will be an end of the war.'" CHAPTER XI. HE Duke of Wellington incurred much blame for not having interfered to save the life of Marshal Ney, who, in violation of the capitulation of Paris, was tried and executed by order of that selfish old glutton, Louis the Eighteenth. The 1 Duke, in answer to the Marshal's personal appeal, declared that the capitulation was a purely military convention between the Allied Commanders and the Prince d'Eckmahl, and did not bind the Government of the King of France. We consider this position untenable, but it is only fair to credit the Duke with sincerity and a belief that he was right.

In his private capacity, the Duke *did,* according to Captain Gronow, use all his influence to save the Marshal. Captain Gronow says: — " The Duke of Wellington was accused of being implicated in the military murder of Ney. Now, so far from this being the truth, I know positively that the Duke of Wellington used every endeavour to prevent this national disgrace; but the Church party, ever crafty and ever ready to profit by the weakness and passions of humanity, supported the King in his moments of excited revenge. It is a lamentable fact, but no less historical truth, that the Roman Catholic Church has ever sought to make the graves of its enemies the foundations of its power. The Duke of Wellington was never able to approach the King or use his influence to save Marshal Ney's life; but everything he could do was done, in order to accomplish his benevolent views."

In a curious old book, called 'The Memorable Battle of Waterloo, &c, &c. ,' by Christopher Kelly, published in 1817, and to which we have been much indebted in preparing the present work, we find an anecdote about the Duke of Wellington which, to us, at all events, is quite new:—

"In the year 1806, the Duke of Wellington (then Sir Arthur Wellesley), after totally routing the Indian chief, Holkar, on the plains of Laswarree, took his passage for England, on board the Company's ship, Lady Jane Dundas. When the anchor was dropped at St. Helena, two boats put off from the ship, as usual crowded with passengers desirous of viewing the island. The boat which conveyed the illustrious warrior, when about a hundred yards from the shore, was upset by one of those sudden squalls blowing from the valleys which are very common at St. Helena. Two men and a boy were instantly drowned; the rest, among whom was our hero, kept struggling with the waves. The moment the accident happened, the boat in company made towards the scene of distress. Sir Arthur Wellesley, unable to swim, had been once or twice under water; a seaman instantly leaped into the sea, and swam towards the sinking hero, whom he bore in triumph to the shore on his left arm and shoulder. The generous tar was ignorant, at the time, of the rank of the person whom he thus saved; he merely selected him from the rest of the sufferers, because he thought his danger was the most imminent; the others, with the exception of the two men and the boy above mentioned, were picked up by the other boat. On landing his exhausted charge, Jack was rewarded by a cordial shake of the hand from the illustrious hero, six bottles of rum, and a warm invitation to come and see him in England; a visit which the honest tar was too modest and unassuming to pay. The Duke's deliverer has now retired from a seafaring life, and settled in Rotherhithe. His friends banter him with the appellation of the saviour of Europe, which he takes in good part; but he never boasts of his achievement; indeed it is very rare that he can be induced to tell his own story, and when it is wrung from him, it is adorned with all the graces of truth and modesty."

This anecdote may be true in its essence, but there are several objections to its authenticity. In the first place, the Duke returned in 1805, not in 1806, and was a passenger on board the Trident, not the Lady Jane Dundas; secondly, having been at Eton, it is improbable that he was unable to swim.

An equally suspicious story is told by Mr. Kelly about Napoleon,—" As it has been frequently asserted, and as often denied, that Buonaparte once came to England to solicit Government for a commission in the British Army, it may be proper to state that he *was* in England, but the object of his appearance here is not known. He lodged at a house in the Adelphi, in the Strand, and remained in London but a short time. This information was obtained from General Miranda, who asserts that he visited him in England at the time. It is probable that the period when Buonaparte was here was about the middle of the year 1793."

Captain Gronow thus describes Blucher's appearance, habits, and manners at Paris in 1815,—" Marshal Blucher, though a very fine fellow, was a very rough diamond, with the manners of a common soldier. On his arrival at Paris he went every day to the Salon, and played the highest stakes at *rouge-et-noir.* The Salon, during the time that the Marshal remained in Paris, was crowded with persons who came to see him play. His manner of playing was anything but gentlemanlike, and when he lost, he used to swear in German at everything that was French, looking daggers at the croupiers. He generally managed to lose all he had about him, alsoall the money his servant, who was waiting in the ante-chamber, carried. I recollect looking attentively at the manner in which he played; he would put his right hand into his pocket, and bring out several rouleaux of Napoleons, throwing them on the red or the black. If he won the first coup, he would allow it to remain; but when the croupier stated that the table was not responsible for more than ten thousand francs, then Blucher would roar like a lion, and rap out oaths in his native language which would doubtless have met with great success at Billingsgate if duly translated; fortunately, they were not heeded, as they were not understood by the lookers-on."

Kelly tells us that "during his campaigns, he sometimes amused himself by playing with the officers of his staff, to whom he generally returned the sums he might have won. But amongst these was a young Prussian Count, whose growing love of play he was resolved, if possible, to check, though unable to control his own. Having won of him to the amount of three thousand pounds, he sent for him to his tent the next morning, and, after a short lecture on the ruinous consequences of gaming, he said,'You are young enough to profit by the example which the indiscretion of a long life has rendered too habitual in me to be conquered. The money which you lost last night I shall restore with pleasure, on condition that you pledge your honour never to play at any game in future by which you can lose more than one hundred roubles in the course of the night.' This pledge being given, the Marshal put into the hand of his young friend half the sum which he had won, saying, 'The remainder of the money I shall seal up under your name, to be received by you on calling upon me at the expiration of twelve months to complete the redemption of your pledge.'"

It is said that when Blucher, on his visit to England in 1814, surveyed London from the ball of St. Paul's, and saw all its extent and riches at his feet, he exclaimed, with enthusiasm, " My God, what a city to plunder 1" Under such a commander, and animated as they were by the direst feelings of revenge, it may easily be imagined that the discipline of the Prussians during the invasion of France in 1815 was as bad as possible. Indeed, all ranks of that intellectual nation behaved rather like banditti than soldiers.

Such English officers who, in 1815, marched to Paris in the track of the Prussian army, bear testimony to the desolation which everywhere met their eyes. Captain Gronow says,—" On our line of march, whenever we arrived at towns or villages through which the Prussians had passed, we found that every article of furniture in the houses had been destroyed in the most wanton manner; looking-glasses, mahogany bedsteads, pictures, beds and mattresses, had been hacked, cut, half burned, and scattered about in every direction; and on the slightest remonstrance of the wretched inhabitants, they were beaten in a most shameful manner, and sometimes shot." The same officer on entering a farm-house about forty miles from Paris could not discover any living being.

"My servant, who had gone upstairs, however, informed me that the farmer was lying in bed, dreadfully wounded from numerous sabre cuts. I approached his bed, and he appeared more dead than alive; but, on my questioning him, he said that the Prussians had been there the night before, had violated and carried off his three daughters, had taken away his cart-horses and cattle, and, because he had no money to give them, they had tied him to his bed and cut him with their swords across the shin-bones, and left him, fainting from pain and loss of blood. After further inquiries, he told me that he thought some of the Prussians were still in the cellar, upon which I ordered my bat-man to load his musket, struck a light, and, with a lantern, proceeded to the cellar, where we found a Prussian soldier, drunk, and lying in a pool of wine which had escaped from the casks he and his companions had tapped.

"Upon seeing us, he, with an oath in German, made a thrust at my bat-man with his sabre, which was parried. In an instant we bound the ruffian, and brought him at the point of the bayonet into the presence of the poor farmer, who recognized him as being one of the men who had outraged his unfortunate daughters, and who had afterwards wounded him. We carried our prisoner to the Provost-Sergeant, who, in his turn, took him to the Prussian headquarters, where he was instantly shot."

No doubt the punishment was inflicted against the grain of the Prussian officers, and only to keep up appearances before the Duke of Wellington.

Captain Gronow also relates that he "once saw a regiment of Prussians march down the Rue St. Honore" when a line of half-a-dozen hackney coachmen were quietly endeavouring to make their way in a contrary direction; suddenly some of the Prussian soldiers left their ranks, and, with the butt-ends of their muskets, knocked the poor coachmen off their seats."

As a contrast to the above, we give the following extract of a note to Sir William Knollys's translation of the Due de Fezensac's campaign in Russia. Speaking of the pillage of Moscow, Sir William Knollys says:— "This doubtless sounds strange in our ears, brother soldiers, particularly when we call to mind the rigorous forbearance enjoined upon us in the south of France in 1814, and the strict discipline by which it was enforced. Woe to the officer who was tempted to turn his mule loose on a bit of inviting but enclosed pasture; worse still for the soldie'r who appropriated to himself, 'without a consideration,' a piece of bread or an apple!.... In 1814, the translator, a short time before the re-embarkation of his regiment for England, on the Gironde was quartered with his company (100 strong) in a capacious chateau in the neighbourhood of Bordeaux, where they remained three days. It was the residence of an extensive wine producer, and had a proportionably extensive cellar. The walls of the long store were lined by a double range of imposing sentries, in the shape of at least 100 barrels of claret. Well kept grounds and an amply stocked garden added to the attractions of the quarter.

"The family had quitted this peaceful abode apparently in some haste, and we may believe under some misapprehension; yet a single servant left in charge seemed to evince a degree of confidence in the uninvited guests. On reconnoitring the premises, the books and music strewed about one of the sitting-rooms, betrayed not only a hurried departure, but the sex, studies, and refined amusements of its late occupants.

"One thought probably crossed officers and men (and somehad seen rough work)as they took leave of such agreeable quarters—it was the gratification their invisible hosts would experience on their return at finding not one article displaced, not a flower missing, not even a cabbage stalk without its head. The stately line of sentries remained in their original close order, intact and entire. What a fearful contrast met the eyes of some of the same party as, on its route to Paris, in the following year, it marched in rear of the Prussian army."

We cannot better conclude this little work than with an extract from Kelly on the subject of the wounded horses at Waterloo:—

"The horses, when wounded in battle, stop short, tremble violently, and groan deeply, while their eyes express a wild astonishment. An officer's horse, which survived the battle of Waterloo, still retains a lively recollection of the wounds sustained on this occasion; the clamour and bustle of the engagement seem to have perpetuated themselves in his ears. When any one approaches him in the stable, he puts himself on the alert for a charge, and starts as if to avoid a sabre cut. Some of the horses, as they lay on the field, having recovered from the first agony of their wounds, began eating the grass around them, thus surrounding themselves with a circle of bare ground, the narrow extent of which demonstrated their weakness. Others of these interesting animals were observed quietly grazing in the middle of the field, between the two hostile lines, their riders having been previously shot off their backs."

E. *J.* FRANCIS AND CO., TOOK'S COURT AND WINE OFFICE COURT, E.C

People of every age, taste, and class, take delight in reading of feats of heroism, dangers bravely encountered, and perils nobly overcome. Messrs. Dean & Son, therefore, are now publishing a series of such narratives in a cheap and popular form. The Series will be entitled the *"DEEDS OF DARING LIBRARY,"* AND THE AUTHOR WILL BE MAJOR KNOLLYS, F.R.G.S., 93rd Sutherland Highlanders,

Author of "Oswald Hastings, or the Adventures of a Queen's Aide-de-Camp;" Joint Author, with Viscountess Combermere, of *"The Life of Field Marshal, Viscount Combermere,"* &c. &c.

A complete Book will be issued every Month, in a Fancy Wrapper, price One Shilling.

Among those to follow this Book (Shaw the Life Guardsman) tvill be 2— THE EXPLOITS OF LORD COCHRANE. 3— THE VICTORIA CROSS IN THE CRIMEA. 4— ,, ,, INDIA. 5— ,, ,, THE COLONIES, &c. 6— UNDECORATED MILITARY AND NAVAL HEROES. 7— GALLANT SEPOYS AND SOWARS. 8— DARINO DEEDS AFLOAT— ROYAL NAVY. 9— ,, ,, ,, MERCHANT NAVY AND PRIVATEERS. 10—FEMALE HEROISM IN WAR. LONDON: DEAN & SON, PUBLISHERS, 160a, ELEET STREET, E.C. *Well-Selected Presentation Books.* *THREE SHILLING AND SIXPENNY ILLUS-TRATED REWARD AND GIFT BOOKS. Especially worthy of notice for Boys, Girls, r Young Ladies' Some, Every-day, or Sunday Reading. Fully Illustrated. Size, 8vo. crown, full cloth gilt, sides, edges, Src.,-new style.* REMAEKABLE MEN: THEIR LIVES AND ADVENTURES.

By M. S. Cockayne, fully Illustrated. Cloth, full gilt sides and edges. Price 3s. 6d.

MEN OP DEEDS AND DARING. The Story and Lessons of their Lives. By E. N. Marks. Fully Illustrated, cloth, full gUt sides and edges, price 8s. 6d. SAYINGS, ACHIEVEMENTS, and INTERVIEWS of GREAT MEN. By the Author of "Heroines of Our Own Times." Fully Illustrated. Cloth, gilt edges, 3s. 6d.

"These stories of the Lives of Illustrious Men will be found to be prepared with so much care and made so very interesting that these three books are sure to become great favourites in every family where young people love to read; such books as these instruct, elevate, and create a noble spirit and a desire to excel in the sphere of life marked out for them. "—*Oxford Times.* OAKFIELD GRANGE. A Tale of School Life for Boys. By Thomas Simmons. Cloth gilt, gilt edges, 3s. 6d.

BOOK OF WONDERS, EVENTS, AND DIS-COVERIES. Edited by John Timbs,

Author of "Things not Generally Known," &c. Fully Illustrated, cloth, full gilt sides and edges, 3s. 6d. ONE HUNDRED and FIFTY BIBLE PICTURES and STORIES.

By Mrs. Upcher Cocsens, Author of "Pleasant Sundays," Editor of "Happy Sundays," &c. Fully Illustrated, cloth, gilt edges, 3s. 6d.

NOTABLE WOMEN; the STORY OF THEIR LIVES. ByE.C. Clayton. Illustrated, cloth, full gilt sides and edges, 3s. 6d.

WOMEN OF THE REFORMATION: THEIR LIVES, TRAITS, AND TBIA1S. By Ellen C Clayton. Fully Illustrated, cloth, full gilt sides and edges, 3s. 6d. CELEBRATED WOMEN. A Book for Young Ladies. By Ellin C. Clayton. Handsomely bound, cloth, gilt edges, 3s. 6d. MINISTERING WOMEN. Edited by Dr. Ctjmmino. Cloth, gilt edges, 3s. 6d. TWO THOU-SAND POUNDS REWARD. A, Tale of London Life. By Elizabeth Melville. With Eight Illustrations by the Author. Cloth gilt, 3s. 6d. DEAN & SON, PUBLISHERS AND FACTORS, 1C0A, FLEET STREET, E. C.

Manufacturer of Valentines, Christmas, Birthday, and Easter Cards,

WELL-SELECTED PRESENTATION BOOKS. HAPPY SUNDAYS FOR THE YOUNG AND GOOD. Fifty-two

Tales for Sunday Reading, in which the Type will be found large, the Illustrations many, the Reading such as should be placed in the hands of a Christian child. In two series, twenty-six Tales in each. Dedi cated to the Rev. R. Bickersteth, late Bishop of Ripon, 3s. 6d.

LIFE AND FINDING OF Dr. LIVINGSTONE. Containing the Original Letters written by H. M. Stanley; with an account of Dr Livingstone's Death, also his Latest Discoveries. Cloth gilt, numerous Illustrations, Portraits, &c, 3s. 6d. DADDY'S MAKINGS. A Comic Rhyming Verse Book, full of original Pictures in colours, by Daddy Dumkins, 3s. 6d.

A Capital Clever Collection of Mirthful Games, Parlour Pastimes, Shadow-Plays, Magic, Conjuring, Card Tricks, Fireworks, Chemical Surprises, &c. Compiled by C. Gilbert. Illustrated by George Cruikshank and others. Cloth gilt, 3s. 6d.

A grand and most curious Collection of Conundrums, Speaking and Acting Charades, Enigmas, Rebuses, Double Acrostics, Picture Proverbs, and Pictorial Hieroglyphics, Square Words, Puzzling Pictures, &c, &c. By Frederick D'arros Planche. Illustrated by George Cruikshank and others, 3s. 6d.

JOLLY GAMES FOR HAPPY HOMES: To amuse our Girls and our Boys, the dear little Babies, and grown-up Ladies. Compiled by G. C. Clark Illustrated. Price 3s. 6d. cloth gilt.

A companion to "Guess Me." and "Endless Mirth." FAMILY FAIRY TALES. Edited by Cholmondeley Pennell, author of "Puck on Pegasus," &c, adorned with beautiful Pictures. This volume has been universally praised by the critical press. 3s. 6d.

NUGENT'S TWELVE COUNTRY-HOUSE CHARADES. Care has been taken to limit the number of the performers to half-a-dozen or thereabouts, and little or no scenery is required. Full music is given with two of the charades should they wish to be performed. 3s. 6d. DRAWING-ROOM PLAYS AND PARLOUR PASTIMES. By

E. L. Blanchard, W. S. Gilbert, J. P. Simpson, Tom Hood, C Smith, Reece, J. C. Brough, A. Sketchley, &c. Collected by Clement Scott, Esq. Price 3s. 6d.

DEAN & SON, PUBLISHERS AND FACTORS, 160A, FLEET STREET, B.C.

Manufacturers of Valentines, Christmas, Birthday, and Easter Cards.

"DANDY," the property of H.R.H. the PRINCESS OF WALES.

DOGS: THEIR POINTS, WHIMS, INSTINCTS, AND PECULIARITIES Edited by H. Webb, assisted by J. dimming Macdona, and other distinguished Prize Winners and Experienced Judges. Price 5s.; or, with sixty Photographs of Prize Winners and Index, Is. 6d. extra. *The Members of the Mastiff Breeding Club, in Council, determinti that the Chapter by Mr. Wtnn, be the standard of points in breeding Mastiffs.* 'The Editor has succeeded in doing what he professed to do, and that is more than can be said about the work of many editors Having

said that Mr. Webb has carried out his programme to the letter, what remains for us here is the recommendation that admirers of the canine race should purchase the book. They will not regret the trifling invest ment."—*The Sportsman.*

" Tells a good deal about the points, whims, instincts, and peculiarities of dogs and many things worth knowing may be learnt from its perusal "—*The Army and Navy Gazette.*

Most exhaustive and amusing, Dr. Gordon Stables on

Gats: Their POINTS AND CHARACTERISTICS: pjATS, with coloured Portraits of Prize Winners.

QATS, with Curiosities of Cat life.

£JATS, their Points and Varieties.

QATS, how to Train, teach Tricks, &c.

£JATS, authenticated Anecdotes.

QATS, how to exhibit to obtain Prizes.

Dr. Stables' Work must be read with pleasure by all. Cloth gilt, 7s.

"The book is a good one, and written with a good knowledge of the subject and with a kindliness of thought and expression which is very pleasing to read. The medical advice is, perhaps, the most valuable oortion of its pages." — *Land and Water,* August 8th.

DEAN & SON, PUBLISHERS AND FACTORS, I60A, FLEET STREET, B.C.

Manufacturers of Valentines, Christmas, Birthday, and Easter Cards, «§ttttn. » nrf Stales. Debrett's Handbooks to the Aristocracy, *Are the cheapest and most reliable Works of the kind, and supply more information of Living Members of the Nobility and the immediate family connections than all other kindred Publications combined.* PUBLISHED ANNUALLY DEBRETT'S ILLUSTRATED PEERAGE and BARONETAGE, WITH TITLES OF COURTESY AND BIOGRAPHICAL KNIGHTAGE.

Complete in one vol., I350 pages, I500 Heraldic Illustrations. Koyal aper, with good margin, half-bound leather, gilt and gilt edges, 2Is.; alf-calf, full gilt sides, 25s.

"For more than a century the name of *Debrett* has been associated with the peerage of this country, and has obtained a reputation for accuracy which

is not surpassed by any work of the kind."—*The Observer.* 'The special characteristics of *Debrett* is that it supplies more information anent of living members of the titled aristocracy than all other kindred works combined."—*Graphic. OB IN TWO VOLUMES, BOUND IN CLOTH, VIZ:—* DEBRETT'S ILLUSTRATED PEERAGE AND TITLES OF COTJETESY of Great Britain and Ireland. Published annually (Jan.) 7I2 pages, cloth gilt, I0s. 6d.j half-calf and gilt edges, I2s.

Contains complete Biographies of the Royal Family and Peers of the Blood Koyal; the Peers and Peeresses of the United Kingdom, with Date of the Creation of the Peerage; the Lords Spiritual; the Heir Apparent oi Heir Presumptive of each Peer or Peeress; the Dowager Lady of any Peer; Peers and Peeresses recently deceased, whose Peerages have become extinct, and Biographical Sketches of every Younger Son or Married Daughter of a Peer, alphabetically arranged; with Seats, Residences, Clubs, etc., of the Royal Family and Peers of the Blood Royal; of every Peeress of the United Kingdom; of the Lords Spiritual, and of every Heir Apparent or Heir Presumptive of each Peer or Peeress of the United Kingdom; and Illustrations of the Armorial Insignia, with Heraldic description of the Royal Family and Peers of the Blood Royal, of the Sees held by the Lords Spiritual and of the Peers and Peeresses of the United Kingdom, and of the Orders of Knighthood. Debrett's Peerage also contains, Alphabetically arranged, the Surname of every Peer and Peeress of the United Kingdom; the Subordinate and Minor Titles of Peers and Peeresses of the United Kingdom, and the Title of every Peer on the Roll of the House of Lords; the Church Patronage, with names of the Livings, and the Correct Translation, in English, of the Mottoes of each Peer, &c. &c.; illustrated with over 700 Illustrations.

"A work which is reasonable in price, not unwieldy in size, and which contains all the information which can be required in a volume of so special a character."—*The Times. 11* Debrett with its 100,000 facts is as free from errors as a work of this description can be. A considerable amount of expense and trouble has been necessary in the production of these volumes, but the exceptional features therein contained will make them increasingly popular."— *Court Journal.* BEAN & SON, PUBLISHERS AND FACTORS, l6i)A, FLEET STREET, B.C.

Manufacturers of Valentines, Christmas, Birthday, and Easter Cards.

DEBKETT'S HANDBOOKS TO THE ARISTOCRACY.

DEBRETT'S ILLUSTRATED BARONETAGE., WITH" THE KNIGHTAGE. Published annually (Jan.) 648 pages, cloth gilt, 10s. 6d.; half-calf and gilt edges, I2s.

Contains complete Biographies of every Baronet and Knight of the United Kingdom: of the Heir Apparent or Heir Presumptive of every Baronet, and of the Dowager Lady of every Baronet and Knight; the Name and Titles of the Predecessors of each Baronet: the Seats, Residences, Clubs, etc., of every Baronet and Knight and the Heir Apparent or Heir Presumptive of each Baronet; the Date of the Creation of each Baronetage; the Coats of Arms of every Baronet, with Heraldic description; the Church Patronage of every Baronet, with Names of the Livings; the Translation into English of the Mottoes of each Baronet; Interesting Anecdotes relating to the Family, and over 750 Illustrations.

"In all the branches of this useful publication there is ample evidence of the painstaking care that has been bestowed upou it by its compilers."—*The Times.*

"The fact that *Debrett* has flourished for 170 years puts it beyond competition; and looking at its completeness, accuracy, and cheapness, we see no room or reason for the appearance of any rust."—*The Echo.* ' *Debrett* is the patriarch of such works. Its special claim to attention is that it aims chiefly at supplying information respecting living members of the aristocracy. The editor judiciously omits all notice of pedigrees, since these are so amply provided for by others. Only first, second, and

third generations are referred to, but the details respecting these are very i.mple, while those portions relating to the younger branches of peers and baronets are unique. Even the addresses are given of the widows of peers, baronets, and knights."—*Morning Post.* DEBRETT'S HERALDIC AND BIOGRAPHICAL HOUSE OP COMMONS AND THE JUDICIAL BENCH. Published annually (Jan.) with 1400 Coats of Arms. Cloth gilt, 7s.; half-bound calf, gilt edges, I0s. 6d.

Contains a full Biography of every Member of Parliament, with Particulars of his Political Views; his arms fully emblazoned and described; his Issue, Residences, Clubs, *Church* Patronage, etc.; Biographies of the Judges of the Superior Courts of England and Ireland, the Scottish Lords of Session, the Commissioners of Bankruptcy, the Recorders, and Judges of the County Courts; the Counties, Cities, and Boroughs Returning Members, with the Names of their Representatives, and Number of Electors; a Dictionary of Parliamentary Phrases; the Name and Address of each Peer or Peeress, etc. ; Translations of all Heraldic Mottoes, and many interesting Tables and Matter not to be found in any other books.

"Very carefully compiled, and will be found a very useful and trustworthy book of reference."—*Standard.* "It contains not only biographical notices of the new members, but a record of the recent Ministerial appointments as welL The division devoted to the Judicial Bench contains biographical sketches of the Judges of the Superior Courts, of County Courts, and of Recorders The book is full of useful information, and is valuable as containing much that the most experienced will find worthy a reference."—*Daily Newt.* DEAN «t SON, PUBLISHERS AND FACTORS, 160A, FLEET STREET, E.C.

Manufacturers oj Valentines, Christina, Birthday, and Easter Cards.

CORNER'S HISTORIES.

CORNERS (Miss) HISTORIES. COMMENCING WITH THE EARLIEST PERIOD OF AUTHENTIC RECORD, AND BROUGHT DOWN TO THE PRESENT TIME. CORNER'S HISTORY OF ENGLAND

AND WALES.

CORNER'S HISTORY OF FRANCE. CORNER'S HISTORY OF GERMANY. CORNER'S HISTORY OF GREECE. CORNER'S HISTORY OF IRELAND. CORNER'S AND KITTO'S SCRIPTURAL HISTORY SIMPLIFIED. ADAPTED FOR YOUTH, SCHOOLS AND FAMILIES,

Of which nearly 200,000 Volumes have been sold.

Uniformly printed, each country in a separate volume; with Illustrations from Historical Subjects, elegantly engraved on Steel, from designs by Sir John Gilbert, J. Franklin, Sec, and an accurate Map to each Volume: well bound in cloth gilt, and lettered.

Miss Cornhr in the composition of these Histories has made it a main object to narrate the principal facts of History in such a clear and-simple manner as to bring them at once within the comprehension of the rising generation without destroying that interest which is suited to readers of a more advanced age; great care has been taken throughout the whole works to avoid as much as possible too tedious a detail of wars and politics, which serve to confuse and fatigue without interesting the youthful mind. There is much in History to delight as well as to instruct; and. as these volumes are written for the amusement and instruction of those who desire to know something about the world they live in, the political history of each state is combined with an account oi its progress in the art of civilization, its natural productions, the social habits of its people at different periods, and all that is most useful and entertaining with regard to their customs, manners, laws, and government.

Miss Corner ventures to assure her readers that they will find the history of a country and its people quite as amusing as any fictitious tale, and far more interesting, because it is true.

CORNER'S HISTORY OF SCOTLAND, from the Earliest Period to the Present Time. By Miss Corner. With Chronological Table, Index, and modern Map. Three full-page Engravings on steel, from paintings by Sir John Gilbert, R.A. Cloth lettered. 2s. 6d. The same Book with Questions for Examination. 8s. "We have perused this history with much interest, delighted with the ease and perspicuity of the style and with the clearness and force of the narrative. "—*Edinburgh Chronicle.* DEAN & SON, PUBLISHERS AND FACTORS, 160a, FLEET STREET, E.C. CORNER'S HISTORY OF SCOTLAND. CORNER'S HISTORY OF ITALY. CORNER'S HISTORY OF HOLLAND AND BELGIUM.

CORNER'S HISTORY OF ROME. CORNER'S HISTORY OF SPAIN AND PORTUGAL.

COBNEB'S HISTOBIES. CORNER'S RISTORY OP ENGLAND AND WALES, from the Earliest Period to the Present Time. Adapted to Youth, Schools, am' Families. By Miss Corner. New Edition, revised and greatly ex tended, by the late Editor of the "English Journal of Education.' Strongly and handsomely bound in cloth, lettered, and contains— (i) Steel Engravings from designs by eminent artists, and a Map ol England and Wales (size 18in. by 14in.,) also (ii) A Pictorial Genealogy of the Monarchs of England, from the Conquest to the year 1857, with graphic illustrations of Remarkable Events (size 32in. by 24in.,) also (Hi) Map of the Costumes, Ships, and Furniture of the various Ages in England, also (iv.) Chronological Table and Index from B.C. 55, also (v.) Table of English Sovereigns, their relationship and progeny, and Lineal descent of Queen Victoria from Egbert, first King of England.

Strongly bound, cloth gilt. 3s. 6d.

The same Cook with Questions for Examination. 4s.

Over *ninety thousand* copies of this work have been sold. The press generally has spoken highly of it, recommending it strongly for school and home use; and the testimony of experienced teachers proves that it is a work which merits the praise bestowed on it.

CORNER'S HISTORY OF IRELAND, from the Earliest Period to the Present Time. By Miss Corner. New Edition, enlarged and improved, with Chronological Table, modern Map and Engravings on steel, from painting by Sir John Gilbert, R.A. Cloth lettered. 2s. 6d. The same

Book with Questions for Examination. 3s.

"The historical facts, always correct, are detailed in plain and concise language. This Is one of the best class-books on Ireland for young people."—*Limerick Stundard.* CORNER'S HISTORY OF FRANCE, from the Earliest Period to the Present Time. By Miss Corner. New edition, enlarged and improved, with Chronological Table, Index, and Map, and scale of British miles and French leagues. Two steel Engravings, finely executed by Davenport, from drawings by J. Franklin. Cloth lettered. 2s. 6d. The same Book with Questions for Examination. 3s.

For eight centuries the history of England has been incidentally connected with that of Ffance; and the history of France is in no small degree the history of modern civilization. A sale of nearly thirty thousand has been realized of this history.

CORNER'S HISTORY OF GERMANY, from the Earliest Period to the Present Time. By Miss Corner. A new Edition, revised and enlarged, with Chronological Table, Index, and Questions for Examination, to which reference is made by figures in the text. An accurate Map, and finely-executed steel Engravings by Davenport, from paintings by Sir John Gilbert, R.A. Cloth lettered. 3s. "We do not know of a more agreeable or instructive present for Youth."—*Times.* DEAN & SON, PUBLISHERS AND FACTORS, 160a, FLEET STREET, E.C. *Manufacturers oj Vaientines, Christmas, Birthday, and Easter Cards.* CORKER'S HISTORIES. CORNER'S HISTORY OF GREECE, from the Earliest Period to the Roman Conquest, with a sketch of its Modern History to the Present Time. By Miss Corner. New Edition, with Questions to each Chapter. Map by Becker, Chronological Table and Index. Cloth lettered. 3s. "This work is ably written. An immense amount of information is given perspicuously and interestingly, the best authorities have been consulted, aud the results of their labours have been judiciously employed by Miss Cornsr."—*Spectator,* CORNER'S HISTORY OP ITALY, from the Earliest Period to

the Present Time. By Miss Corner. New Edition. Cloth gilt, steel-plate Engravings, from designs by Sir John Gilbert, R. A., and Map. 2s. 6d. Italy is now, in an historical point of view, one of the most interesting kingdoms in existence.

"Written with great care and ability."— *John Bull,* CORNER'S HISTORY OP HOLLAND AND BELGIUM, from the Earliest Period to the Present Time. By Miss Corner. With a Map and Steel-plate Engravings, from designs by Sir John Gilbert, R.A. Cloth gilt. 2s. 6d.

"A condensed mass of knowledge, well put together, and well illustrated. "—*Church and State Gazette.* CORNER'S HISTORY OF ROME, from the. Earliest Period to the Close of the Empire. Adapted to Youth, Schools, and Families. By Miss Corner. With Map of the Empire, Chronological Table, and Index. Questions subjoined to each Chapter. Constant Reference to Authorities. Cloth lettered. 3s. 6d. "Miss Corner's History of Rome is well written, and the historical facts elicited by the learned labours of Niebuhr, Arnold, &c, are made to take the place of the fabulous accounts which have hitherto passsd current as authentic history; at the same time the popular early leg-ends are Dot omitted, but their doubtful nature is pointed out."— *Westminster Review.* CORNER'S HISTORY OF SPAIN AND PORTUGAL, from the Earliest Period to the Present Time. By Miss Corner. Map of Spain and Portugal. Fine steel Engravings, from drawings by J. Franklin. New Edition, enlarged and improved. Cloth lettered. 2s. 6d. The same Book with Questions for Examination. 3s. "The advantage of publishing these two histories in one volume will be apparent to every teacher. Miss Corner has been singularly fortunate in making this volume one of the most pleasing of her historical library. There are but few school histories of Spain and Portugal, and it is not too much to say that there is not one written in so interesting and accurate a manner as this."—*Daily News.* "So concise and plain as to be at once adapted to the capacities and volatility of young people, while they are useful compendiums for adults."—*Times.* CORNER AND

KITTO'S SCRIPTURAL HISTORY SIM PLI-FIED; in Questions and Answers, for the use of Schools and Families. By Miss Corner. Revised by John Kitto, D.D., F. S.A. New Edition, with Chronological Table, Index, and two Maps, one to illustrate the early part of Scripture History. Cloth boards. 3s. 6d. Dr. Kitto co-operated with Miss Corner in writing this work, and the testimony which he bore to her ability is most satisfactory. He wrote: "The authoress has shown great skill and judgment in the condensation of large statements and seizing the salient points of the subject before her." DEAN & SON, PUBLISHERS AND FACTORS, 160a, FLEET, STREET, E.C. *Manufacturers of Valentines, Christmas, Birthday, and Easter Cards.*

Corner's Juvenile Historical Library. *These little Histories are rendered pleasing to young children, and are adapted to their capacities, so that the principal facts may be known without their minds being burdened with unimportant details.* COBNER'S EVERY CHILD'S HISTORY OF ENGLAND, from the Earliest Period to the Present Time. By Miss Corner. New Edition, stiff cover, uncoloured Map. Is.

Same Book bound in cloth, coloured Map; *Portraits of the Monarch, and Events to be Remembered.* Is. 6d. History for children ought to be told in their own simple language, or it fails to interest them; while all that is unfitted for childish cars, or unsuited to a childish understanding, should be carefully omitted. I have allotted a distinct period for the subject of every chapter, and have arranged a Series of Questions at the end of each, to render my History useful as a School-book for the junior classes.—Julia Corner. CORNER AND PARR'S EVERY CHILD'S HISTORY OP FRANCE, from the Earliest Period to the Present Time. Examination Questions are subjoined to each chapter. With Map of France. Stiff covers. Is.

The same Book, with Portraits of upwards of Seventy of the Sovereigns of Franco. Cloth. Is. 6d.

CORNER AND PARR'S EVERY CHILD'S HISTORY OP GREECE. With Map of Greece, and Questions for Examination to each chapter. Stiff covers. Is. The same Boot, cloth bound. Is. 6d. "So cleverly has Miss Corner used the excellent materials at her disposal, that her History is at once a stepping-stone for the young pupD, a summary for the general reader, and a compendium for the student. To write an abridgment of such a book is a task in the art of *precis* writing. Dr. Farr undertook the task, and it is but justice to him to say that he has performed it most creditably."—*English Journal of Education.* CORNER AND PARR'S EVERY CHILD'S HISTORY OF ROME, from the Earliest Period to the Decline of the Roman Empire.

With Map. Stiff covers. Is.

The same Book, cloth, Is. 6d.

This Book has been described by the Press as "the best stepping-stone to the best

School History of Rome." From the testimony of teachers and parents, the publishers believe that this description conveys a well deserved compliment to Miss Corner and to Dr. Farr.

CORNER AND KITTO'S EVERY CHILD'S SCRIPTURE

HISTORY. Two Maps; viz., Wanderings of the Children of Israel from Egypt to the Promised Land, and Palestine _in the Time of our

Saviour. Stiff covers. Is.

The same Book, cloth, Is. 6d.

This Book, like that from which it was adapted, has been highly commended in most of the religious newspapers and magazines. It is not compiled in the catechetical form, but

Examination Questions are appended to each section.

CORNER, RODWELL AND PARR'S CHILD'S FIRST STEP

TO THE HISTORY OF ENGIAND, by Rodwell. New Edition, revised and corrected. Illustrated with Portraits of the Sovereigns and

Map of England. Chronological Table and Principal Events to be

Remembered in each page. Cloth gilt. 2s. 6d.

DEAN & SON, PUBLISHERS AND FACTORS, 160A, FLEET, STREET, B.C. JUVENILE EDUCATIONAL BOOKS. *The Books in this series generally, are stepping-*

stones *from the nursery to the school-room, being written in a pleasant manner, and are sure to amuse while they instruct; the greater number are well illustrated. The seven dark squares out of the ten represent water; the other three, white, the lands this will show you, exactly, how much greater is the proportion of water than land.* Quotation, showing-the simple manner in which Geography is explained by Miss Saroeant, in PAPA AND MAMMA'S EASY LESSONS IN GEOGRAPHY; or, the Elements of Geography in a new and attractive form. By Anna Maria Sarqeant. Fully Illustrated. Price Is. in stiff covers; or, Is. 6d. bound in cloth, gilt. The object of Miss Sarqeants little book is not only to induce children to like Geography, but also to impart in a simple and attractive manner, elementary knowledge of the subject: in other words, a good and complete groundwork. The book is written in an amusing dialogue form and is illustrated with numerous explanatory engravings, and is intended as a companion book to Miss Corner's "Play Grammar." CHARLES BUTLER'S YOUNG PUPIL'S EASY GUIDE TO GEOGRAPHY. For the use of Schools and Private Instructors. New Edition, enlarged, modernized and re-arranged by Dr. R. H. Mair. Strongly bound in cloth. Is. 6d. This adaptation of a school book which has for so many years been a favourite amongst teachers and pupils, will, it is hoped, give general satisfaction. Dr. R. H. Mair has carefully revised the book. To each chapter is appended a series of Questions. A copious Index, with reference to upwards of eleven hundred places, is also appended.

"This is truly what it professes to be, an Easy Guide. We recommend it without hesitation."—*Athenarum.* CHARLES BUTLER'S GUIDE TO GEOGRAPHY, WITH THE

USE OF THE GLOBES. By Charles Butler, re-arranged by Dr. K.

H. Mair. Price 2s. strongly bound in red cloth, gilt.

This work is comprised of the "Young Pupil's Guide to Geography, Butler's Use of

the Globes," and seven Glyphographic

Maps.

CHARLES BUTLER'S GUIDE TO USEFUL KNOWLEDGE.

Containing, in the form of a familiar Catechism a variety of information connected with the Arts, Sciences, and Phenomena of Nature. For the use of Schools and Private Instructors. By Charles Butler. New Edition, revised and corrected throughout by G. Martin. Cloth, embossed, price Is. 6d. This work is in itself a simple yet comprehensive cyclopaedia of general information. It describes Articles of consumption used chiefly as food and drinks; articles used for flavouring food, as spices, &c. Vegetable and animal productions used in the arts, and their applications; Earths, stones, &c. as applied to the arts; Materials from which are obtained colours and dyes; Chemistry; Miscellaneous inventions; Electricity, galvanism, electric telegraph, &c. &c. There is an index to about 1000 different items.

DEAN & SON, PUBLISHERS AND FACTORS, 100a, FLEET STREET. E.C. JUVENILE EDUCATIONAL BOOKS. THE PLAY GRAMMAR; or, ELEMENTS OP GRAMMAR EXPLAINED IN EASY GAMES, RIDDLES, &c. By Miss Corner. New Edition, 40th thonsand, enlarged and improved. Numerous woodcuts. Coloured frontispiece and title: cloth bound, price Is. 6d.; or, with tinted frontispiece and title, and in stiff covers, Is.

This Grammar is a great improvement on the tedious dry catechisms of grammar, which are the dread of children. Too much is not attempted; the science of language is not generally attractive to children, unless conveyed in a plain and easy style.

Specimen of the style in which the Illustrations are introduced to assist the child in understanding Grammar.

Miss Corner's "Play Grammar" is heyond all comparison the best contrivance we have seen for teaching this difficult science to young children."—*Reader.* ROUND GAMES AND AMUSING EXERCISES UPON GRAM MAR. An Addendum to Corner's Play Grammar and all other

Grammars. Forty woodcuts. Price Is.

This is an amusing companion to all grammars for the young. It is a capital collection of rhymes, conundrums, and *jeux* relative te grammar. It renders grammar not only *easy,* but really and truly amusing."—*Critic.* THE GRADUATED ENGLISH GRAMMAR. No. 3, of Dean And Son's Illustrated School Books. Forty-two pages, large 8vo., stiff cover, price 4d.

This is one of the cheapest and best English Grammars published. Those points on which grammarians differ have been studied so as to bring out the leading sense of their views, and the utmost care has been taken to secure accuracy, according to the best and newest authorities on the language. The Questions are carefully graduated, and the Exercises will be found very serviceable to the learner.

NOAH WEBSTER'S ENGLISH AND AMERICAN ILLUSTBATED SPELLING AND BEADING BOOK. For the use of Schools and Families. Upwards of 150 Engravings illustrative of the lessons. Large 8vo. strongly bound in cloth, lettered. Price Is.

This is really a *progressive* Spelling and Reading Book. The lessons are easily graduated from the Alphabet and combinations of two letters to the longest words in the English, language. It is arranged in three Parts, Part I. is adapted for very young children, and is a great improvement on most arrangements. Part II. is mostly in words of two syllables. Part III. is in words of three or more syllables, and contains a larger amount of useful information and moral instruction than is usually conveyed in spelling books and elementary reading books.

DEAN & SON, PUBLISHERS AND FACTORS, Igoa, FLEET STREET, E.C. JUVENILE EDUCATIONAL BOOKS. DEAN'S ILLUSTRATED MODERN SPELLING AND READING BOOK. Containing the information of Carpenter, with the usefulness of Butter, and the simplicity of Mavor. Strongly bound in embossed cloth, lettered, Is. 6d. The definitions to the words are clear and concise, and the book is printed on good paper, and in beautifully clear type. It is embellished

with upwards of eighty explanatory Engravings to its immense amount of miscellaneous information, conveyed in a most attractive way.

FIRST BOOK OF SPELLING AND READING, No. X, of

Dean's Illustrated School Books. Thirty-two pages, large 8vo. Fifty Engravings. Price 4d.

SECOND BOOK OF SPELLING AND READING, Book No. 2, of Dean's Illustrated School Books. Thirty-two pages, large 8vo. Forty-three Engravings, price 4d.

THE ROYAL NURSERY A, B, C, AND FIRST BOOK; being Book I. Of Wholesome, Light, And Sweet Educational Food Fob The Yoonq; Illustrated with above 400 pictures of every-day objects, most familiar to Childhood, and clock face with moveable hands, to teach children the time. Crown 8vo. sthT covers, 6d. THE ROYAL NURSERY SPELLING AND READING BOOK; being Book II. Of Wholesome, Light, And Sweet Educational Food; with above 250 pictures of every-day common and familiar objects, including lessons in colouring, with 58 illustrations. Same size as

Book I. price 6d.

The Two Books, I, and II. bound together, price Is. It may be truly asserted, that this is one of the best First Books ever published. The numerous illustrations, (over 400 in Book I. and 250 in Book II.) are of great importance, tending not only to amuse, but to impress upon the memory the name and character of the objects and common things intended to be conveyed. By this most gradual and simple process, the child is led on to form an entire sentence, and that easily comprehended, and always of interest. Getting further advanced, the numerous illustrations are severally explained and coloured; hence the knowledge and amusement of the child is greatly increased. The Clock, and idea of numbers, are also admirably taught.

EDUCATIONAL COURSE, FIRST SERIES. THE PRIMER: containing Easy Progressive Lessons in Single Syllables. By the Rev. W. L. Nelson, Head-master of St. Stephen's School, Edinburgh; embellished with upwards of 150 Engravings of familiar and every-day objects. Crown 8vo. in stiff covers, price 6d. THE FIRST READING BOOK, containing Easy Progressive Lessons of Spelling and Beading. By the Rev. W. L. Nelson, Head-master of St. Stephen's School, Edinburgh; profusely illustrated with Engravings of familiar every-day objects. Crown 8vo. stiff covers, 6d. The Two Books bound together in One, price Is, The two last-named books are very neatly got up, with an abundance of pictures of every-day life, the lessons being progressive; and bound in handsome cover in colours. In the second book the more difficult words are placed at the head of each chapter, so that the words may be spelt and understood before commencing to read. DEAN & SON, PUBLISHERS AND FACTORS, 160a, FLEET STREET, E.C. 1 DR. ROOKE'S ANTI-LANCET. WHAT IS IT? / Handy Guide to Domestic Medihie. Every Household should possess a Copy. JR. ROOKE'b Anti-LANCET.

All Invalids should rea'l the Chapter On the I'unctions of Digestion, showing: y Oiai process food is converi Hi utn blood—I low blood sustains the whole system—H w nervous power influences all the hoddv organs to perform their allotted f'mctions—I ri m i pies of life anil death unlolded— Dying' seldom

accompanied with pa n—.Cental vision aim-lined prior t'i tiie death of the bod)— iinmortality of t ie intelligent principle.

DR. ROOKE'S A STI-LANCETS

The Nervous the Dyspeptic, or the Hypochondriuc, should read the Chapter on the Origin of all Diseases from depr ssio" of nervous or vital power — How explaineu—Producing or exciting eauseitfev of ncrvou depression—Efteets of the mind onieJp bod —Effects of excessive joy—Auer—Uriel and suspense — Sudden surprise and Jriiflit— Hani study — Hot relaxing fluids— ut mperauce in eating and drinking— Spirituous liquois— Lost of h ood— huimre air.

DR. ROOKE'S ANTI-LANCET.

Read the Chapter on the Destructive I'ractic of Bleeding, illustrated by the eases of Lord Uvran, ir Walter cott, Madame Malihraii, Count favour. General feStonewaU" Jackson, and other puhlic characters.

CROSBY'S BALSAMIC COU G H EL I X I R. OPIATBS, NARCOTICS, a-d SQ ILLS are too often invoked to give relief in COUGHS, I OLDS, and all PULMONARY DISEASES. Instead of such fallacious remedies, which yield momentary relief at the expense of enfeebling the digestive organs, and thus increasing that debility which lies at the root or the mala-

dy, modern scie ce points to CROSBY'S BALSA vllC COUGH iiLJXlR as the t ue remedy.

Da. ROOKE'S TESTIMONIAL.

Da. Rooxk, Scarborough, author of the "Anti. Lancet," says:—

'confidence, recommend it as a most valuable i

"adjunci to an otherw-se strengthening treat-

'ment lor this disea c.",

"I have repeatedly observed how very rapidly and "invariably it subdued Coiuh, P.iiu, and ir"ritatii n of the Chest in cases of Pulmonary "Consumption, and I can, with the greatest ...... —-j

This medicine, which is free from opium and squills not only allays the local irritation, but improves digestion and strengthens the constitution. Hence it s used vi h the n ost signal success in ASTHMA, CONSUMPTION, INFLUENZA, I CONSUMPTIVE MGHi SWEAIS, BRONCHITIS. COUGHS,) QUI sY. And all affections of the Throat & Cheat

Sold in Bottles, at U 9d., 4a. 6d., and lis. each, by all respectable Chemists, and wholesale by JAMES M. CROSBY, Chemist, Scarborough, England.

V Invalid should read Crosby's Prize Trcati e on "DISEASES CF THE LUNGS AND AIRVESSELS,'' a copy of which can be h id Gratis of all Chemists.